# Ximenes & Other Poems by John William Polidori

John William Polidori was born on 7th September 1795 in London to Gaetano Polidori, an Italian political émigré scholar, and Anna Maria Pierce, an English governess. He was the eldest of 8 children.

From 1804 Polidori was a pupil at the recently formed Ampleforth College. In 1810 he proceeded to the University of Edinburgh, where he wrote a thesis on sleepwalking and received his degree as a doctor of medicine on 1st August 1815. He was 19.

In 1816, Dr. Polidori was given the job of Byron's personal physician and accompanied him on a trip through Europe. The publisher John Murray offered Polidori £500 to keep a diary of their travels. At the Villa Diodati, Byron's rented villa at Lake Geneva in Switzerland, the pair met with Mary Wollstonecraft Godwin, Percy Bysshe Shelley, and Mary's stepsister, Claire Clairmont.

One night in June, after the company had read aloud from a French collection of German horror tales, Byron suggested they each write a ghost story. There were to be two outstanding works from that evening; 'Frankenstein' by Mary Shelley and Polidori's 'The Vampyre' which would be the first published modern vampire story in English.

Dismissed by Byron, Polidori traveled in Italy and then returned to England. His story, 'The Vampyre', was published in the April 1819 issue of New Monthly Magazine without his permission. Much to the annoyance of both Polidori and Byron it was the latter who was credited as author.

Polidori also had published 'Ximenes, The Wreath & Other Poems' in 1819 and his long theological and sacred poem 'The Fall of the Angels' in 1821 as well as two plays, essays and his diary.

Despite his youth Polidori was increasingly worn down by gambling debts and depression.

John William Polidori died on 24th August 1821 at the age of only 25 in London.  Although his death was recorded as death by natural causes, strong evidence asserts that it was suicide by means of cyanide.

I0157795

## Index of Contents

Captive's song
To Italy
Sonnets


PREFACE

Ambition has many ways of advancing towards the pinnacle, from which it hopes to catch fame by the wing, and chain her to its column, though it be even like that of the Ascetic in Thebais. It is the most assuming of all passions. Its appetite, like that of the furnace, indeed, increases with the fuel thrown in, which but raises a greater flame, requiring greater faggots for its continuance. There was a time, when poetry, contented in the sylvan shade, sought but to please.'—Now, since even lords have become desirous of wreathing the bay around their coronet, poetry has dared more,—it has crouched into a footstool for ambition to tread upon while aiming at power.—She has sounded her lyre in the princes' hall, not in laughing merry strains, but in tones that roused the Epicure from his feast, the Cytherean from his couch.

She has uttered from the rocks of Ireland tones that have so awakened sympathy (long overpowered by intolerant bigotry) for the sufferings of warm-hearted brothers, that even Ministers amidst their revels, have started like Belshazar at voices echoed by the very walls. And those notes which she sounded over a Sheridan's bier must have made some shrink, who saw the pointed linger, and heard the scornful lip repeat the verse, wherein talent learns what it may gain from the corruption it adorns.

The' unassuming lay of poetry by addressing the passions, wins the mind that resists the calm attempts of reason. Such, indeed, has been the influence exerted by her sons, that men of talent, who might have been heard in the higher house, pleading the cause of nations, before judges who would have listened with deference to their genius, have rather chosen to gratify their vanity, by exert'd the power and employing the lyre she gave, in causing every heart to thrill, every breast to sigh in unison, with their own often imaginary feelings. The gigantic grief of one noble author, not content with the anguish of the heart he owned, seized upon the lyre and struck its chords; instantly its very note was echoed in the wildest solitude, and sounded in the most crowded hall. What are the gratifications of authority, of power, when compared to this? They cause the scowling look to threaten the power it dreads, or at most gain the obsequious smirk, which tries to cover with deceitful flowers the fall it prepares. Poetry, when she weds herself to man, causes his emotions to be the emotions of all,— makes his soul, as it were, the sentient soul of a world.

The attempt to gain sympathy and influence from others forming the common occupation of all, can it be wondered that one, whose profession offers no route by which even imagination could wend its way to power in the state, should seize upon the lyre? Can it be wondered that one, whose professional honours were acquired at a comparatively early period, should thus occupy the idle moments that precede the attainment of public confidence? After having done all that can be demanded of him, who asks that the life of a parent, a daughter, or a wife, should be entrusted to his care—can it be wondered that he should attach himself to poetry? Poetry was the relaxation he sought for while tracing his path through the unstable sands of metaphysical disquisition and medical theory,—when the one bewildered, and the other misled, it refreshed his way-worn mind, and again prepared him to lose his path. If, even when engaged amidst these studies, poetry did not impede his progress, should it be imputed to him as a sign of neglecting the sacred trust reposed in a physician, that he still at moments takes it up? Idleness to a young active mind, is a poison that proves but too powerful a sapper of the mind's life to be indulged in,—And what is there that can entirely occupy such a mind satisfactorily for years, in the unavoidable moments of relaxation and idleness? Manual exercises pall and tire when once gone through, and when the utmost that one's frame and strength of body will allow to be executed has been discovered: to leap always the same height, to receive the same number of blows at a sparring match, to gain the same number of notches at cricket, to fence, to dance, to ride,— all pall; for when a certain degree of excellence has been gained, the boundary becomes visible, and nothing more remaining to be attained, the ambitious mind droops. Mathematics and positive abstract science, require years of constant uninterrupted study and application before there is even a possibility of going beyond a Newton or a La Place by one thousandth part of their knowledge, and before an individual gains a name like theirs, centuries must elapse, while thousands of martyrs perish in the study, after spending their lives in merely suggesting hints, of which, at last, some more fortunate genius obtains the credit, by merely showing his mastery in the arrangement of the fasces formed from these of themselves weak branches.

Where then to look for a relaxation from the severer duties of attending the poor in sickness, of hearing their complaints in convalescence? History requires so much minute criticism, and sobriety of judgment, as seldom attend the earlier years of man;—and what is at last gained? A physician after one years attendance among the poor, can write as good a treatise upon human folly, passion, and gratitude, as the historian in his study, after turning over for years the same leaves of Muratori or even of the Bollandists. Poetry, however, which seems as the primrose in spring, to be the harbinger of passion in the human life, which all men have felt within their breast, though many have not given it audible expression, offers a relaxation requiring no continuous exertion and no engrossing application;—it can be laid down when severer studies require attention, and resumed when a vacant moment arrives. It offers its aid, alike to soften the exuberance of joy and to sooth the disappointment so constantly attending youthful hopes. It is upon this principle that the author has made poetry his mistress.—It is for the love of fame and for the sake of assertins: a rank above the herd whom, with Horace, odit profanum et arcet, that he has made the whisperings of his mistress public. He does not think that these shall illustrate his name and form the halo that shall adorn his grave, but he hopes that the public will notice them so far as to point out their defects; he then hopes that like the young eagle when the downy plumage of his nest, by the aid of which he first attempted to soar, has fallen, he may employ a stronger pinion, and raise himself whence he may gaze on thousands below himself.

The poems here published were written at different periods of my life.—Ximenes was written in my eighteenth year, the others from that time till the present. I have called Ximenes a dramatic action, though to all intents and purposes it is a tragedy. I do this because I think that tragedy is an improper name; my song is not for the reward of a goat. I might as well call it endoxiody as I sing for fame, or any other compound I might prefer. A dramatic action seems to me to be the preferable title, for it is a narration by action.—Beside which, tragedy implies by use, a poem written for the stage, which idea is quite incompatible with my poem. For Religion in no way, can be a subject for a playhouse audience. Indeed I think the name of God should never be heard within the walls of a theatre. I am aware that instances may be adduced of plays of interest and fame resting entirely on religion, but I am not inclined to bow even to the authority of applause. I think everything united with religion should be preserved for the closet— that not even the powers of superstition in combination with Christianity, should be put into the hands of those who exert their talents for the applause of an audience formed of peers and sailors, prostitutes and senators.

I intended in the Wreath to have painted the progress of love in a young breast, and to have made a poetic youth relate his own story by the verses he is supposed to address to his mistress.—I had intended to have painted many of the lesser colourings which depend upon a frown or a smile, but my pencil failed; I have left the hero wavering between a foreign clime and death, and have brought him to this dilemma, without sufficiently progressive steps towards so dismal an end.—If what I have done please, the world will not lose, for by its smile, I shall be encouraged to proceed—if not, the world will be a gainer by not having to read more before it judges; and I shall have been spared the toil of fatiguing myself, but to give more materials on which my condemnation may be founded.

My Sonnets I fear are not upon many occasions legitimate.—I have introduced a greater variety of metres and rhyming points than are used by the Italians, the masters in this trifle. I might defend the practice by the usage in this country, but it is so trifling a point that I think taking this advantage hardly counterbalances the greater facility of Italian versification. And though many may say with Menzini,

In questo di Procruste orrido letto
Chi ti sforza di giacer?

Yet I have not been dismayed, for there are so many momentary feelings that require some poetic frame, that the disadvantages of sonneteering will be more than compensated, if England can ever boast like Italy of a few poems equal to Petrarch's "Levommi il mio pensier" &c.

A young author must in many cases be a plagiarist, his personal experience is limited—he must therefore copy the feelings of others, and his imagination must fill up the shading where the original has only given the bold outline. Indeed the quantity of poetry is now so great that he must indeed be a gigantic genius who can stride amidst the huge reams of poetic effusions without stumbling over any. Most poets must be content with acting like the sunbeam upon a cloudy day, whose ray piercing in partial gleams through the veil of heaven, merely brings out spots here and there, while the rest is shaded, and thus gives the appearance of something new to a scene which before had often been illuminated with one blaze of light by the orb itself. Thus the inferior poet's mind may claim to itself the merit of throwing out in a more prominent way, some before hidden accessary to the image of a greater poet.

But I started with ridiculing authors, who offered excuses, and here I have been tendering palliatives to the feared abuse of the critics.—I will say no more, than that I am resigned to the fate of my work, as I am not of the opinion of some, that real merit may be trampled upon; if I possess it—it will not be a monthly or even a quarterly review that can deny it with impunity; if I have it not in my possession, not even their praises can save me from the oblivion I merit.


XIMENES

DRAMATIS PERSONÆ
XIMENES
GUSTAVUS
ALMORADDIN
ANSELMO
RINALDO

DOMINIC
EUPHEMIA
MONKS, ATTENDANTS


SCENE: A Grecian Isle


## TO MY BOOK

Go forth, my little book, unto the world
And speak for me;—be banner like unfurl'd
Tore all, to speak thy master's lonely heart.—
Thou art my only hope!—from thee I part
Hoping but visions chance, yet they are all
That rouse me as I list to nature's call,
Which spoken by the breeze hurling the flowers
From their light living stem, e'er heaven lowers.
Tells me that peace is found alone in death.—
But thy new image I have tried to wreathe
With future hopes in such a way, the thought
Begins to dawn, that happiness is bought
By mental toil, if the world's smile but pass
Over the midnight lamp and studious glass.—
I—yes, I must confess, while writing thee
My heart was light, was full of hopes of glee.—
For I have hoped that e'en fair ladies' lip
Might speak my name with praise—that they might dip
Into thy page, whene'er the lover's breath
Did not in wanton whispers speak—when wreath
Of many-coloured flowers fading, thouarb nlaced
By lover's hand midst locks which might have graced
Even —'s form, would seem to say
He had been absent the long weary day.—
Yes, I have thought the world might speak of me,
And with its voice might bid these demons flee
That hang upon my heart, as they would drag
Me down, and make me laughter to that hag
Who, fables tell, can with a glance to stone
Change all men's forms, for she would hear me groan.
And scoff at me, that I refuse to seek
Her sovereign power 'gainst all the pains which wreak
Her vengeance on my soul.—But I can't bow.
My mind wont bend to aught that's here below;
My weary soul though scarr'd in every part.
Yet feels in every scar as if the smart

Arose on feeling's self.

I know I dream.
Thinking thy form can gain immortal gleam
Of fame—but yet a straw is grasp'd when fail
The bough or bush upon the stream, though frail—
And I, who've roamed midst men and seen their haunts
From Borne, which in its very ruin daunts
Oblivion from approach, to where the land.
My native isle! once midst the circling band
Of mists and snows forgotten, now has rais'd
A pinnacle of fame which is not grazed
By any ancient bird of great renown.
Though from the seven hills its flight be flown—
But yet, where'er I've been, have only found
That all was vain, that to all actions bound
Hung misery and grief awaiting all
Who live in peasants' filth, in noble's hall—
Have only heard the poet talk of bliss
As he would fall upon his knees, and kiss.
With lip as wanton as the gods', tlie bough
Pluck'd from the laurel's trunk, while fancy's glow
Threw o'er his form a light, as if a glance
This very God had deigned on him to lance—
I sought these joys, but bliss fled from my grasp.—
Then where to hope this pleasant form to clasp
I know not—save the world's fair word may raise
Such phantoms as deceive, because they praise.

But yet I have my doubts, and think he knew
Mankind, who those two sons while dreaming slew.
For by their acts they had deserv'd his smile
And fondest mother's prayer had asked the while
That he should there his kindest blessing deign.
While none were found his judgment to arraign.
Methinks that death alone affords 'gainst grief
A constant shield to woe unfound relief—
For none have risen to say the worm's tooth pain'd.
And nought from the grave's mouth a groan e'er gain'd,

Yet still, my book, go forth—I will await
And make the hours fly quick—-for in thy fate
I will absorb myself, and chance forget
In thy sad end, those pains that seem to whet
On time their never blunting points.—Farewell.—
Go—go and bid fame forth thy doom to tell.
And if she deck me with her glittering vest,
Though demons revel in my aching breast.

Yet as the ivy mantling o'er the wreck
Of some tough oak, still can for ages deck
Its dead and rotten trunk—so shall her praise
Cause that my smiles deceive those who may pass and gaze.

ACT I

SCENE I

Seem, a solitary Sea Beach.—**XIMENES** alone.

**XIMENES**
Where next will cheating hope direct my way?
Already o'er the land-girt sea I've flown
Impatient of the winds.—But vain has been
My eager search—no tidings can I learn
To fan the lingering half-extinguished spark
Still cherished by my hatred; none can say
Why feelings rise unbidden—why firm hope
So suddenly elates desponding minds—
Else why when first this island's distant shore
Rose dimly on my view—why beat my heart
As with the consciousness that I approached
My toilsome wandering's long-expected goal?—
Sure 'twas unwillingness to part from all
So long desired—so anxiously pursued,—
Once, when with youth my fantasy was warm,
I hung o'er nature's charms, as if myself
Were part thereof—but naught can now arrest
My wandering steps—the sun's benignant smile
Is darkness to my soul—I only breathe
Within the narrow vale bounded by cliffs
High rising to the heavens, and shutting out
The light of day, between whose sides one path
Winds under dark death-frowning rocks—I breathe.
But only breathe—for soon the peasant crowd
With noisy carol echoing through the chasm
Drives me to some remoter wilderness—
Like him of Greece beside the crater's mouth
A solitary dwelling let me raise—
I'll to Vesuvius demons thence, 'tis said,
Breathe their destructive blasts.—There I can gaze
On ruin, and exulting hear the cries
Of mothers, wives, and all that love can name.

When they behold the fiery lava flood
Rolling tremendous o'er their shattered homes,—
For years the toiling swain may tend the vine—
For years the mountain's smiling sides may vest
A richer hue than leaves alone can give—
For years the purple cluster may invite
Unthinking fools to revel—songs of joy
May rise around me, but the foul fiend's mock
Shall mingle with them, as he spreads his snares
And ambushes with death the flow'ry scenes.

[Sounds of chaunting at a distance.

Is there no solitude on earth, that here
E'en here where on the sand is seen no trace
Of human step, the song of man intrudes?
But 'tis a melancholy sound; 'twill be
Some false though loud lament, such as is heard
When o'er a parent's bier some spendthrift son
Arrays the heartless pageantry of grief.—

[Enter a procession of **MONKS** bearing tapers, &c. **GUSTAVUS** in the midst as a penitent.

Nay, has then superstition spread a veil
So thick o'er mortal eyes in every clime
That in this distant island, where methinks
Deluding priests could scarcely hope to thrive,
Its splendid mummeries cajole the weak.
And e'en the noble spirit, as it seems.
Stoops from its native dignity, to be
The dupe and laughing stock—
But what!—bis very lineaments!—tis he!
Francesco!

**GUSTAVUS**
Ah! what voice is that! my name—

[**XIMENES** retires.

Hark! was it not my name?

**MONK**
Your name my Lord—
You only dream, as sometimes you are wont.

**GUSTAVUS**
It may be so; but oft to me the air
Sounds as a distant bell, with threatening toll

Against my crimes—yet others hear it not.

[Exit with the procession.

**XIMENES**
'Tis well; for had I inadvertently
Betrayed myself, then hopeless were revenge.—

[Enter **RINALDO**.

Good friend! a word—if fame belie you not,
You are kind hosts, and strangers all receive
A friendly welcome here, I fain would know
What solemn errand guides yon holy train.

**RINALDO**
You doubtless in the midst perceived a man
Bent down by weight of grief, not worn with age—
His trembling feet could scarcely bear him on.
His haggard eye upon the ground was fixt.
Fearing alike on heaven or man to look.—

**XIMENES**
I noted him— barefoot he trod the ground
With head uncovered and in sackcloth garb.

**RINALDO**
'Tis said, that bound by some mysterious vow,
As each new moon in modest virgin fear
Hides her effulgence from our mortal gaze,
With naked feet he treads the sandy beach.
And spends in yonder church the twofold night—
There rapt in grief he lies upon the sod,
Where death prepares for all a tranquil couch—
With bitter tears invoking peace he lies,
As if to call her from the only seat
She yet has found upon this changeling orb.
Thence he retires to more than hermit's cell.
Where, it is said, he oft is heard at night
Pacing with restless step the narrow floor.
And uttering groans so mournful and so deep
That fiends seem revelling in his maddening pains.

**XIMENES**
But is the cause of this strange grief unknown?

**RINALDO**
There are reports abroad of crimes, but these -

Are hidden.—He has not been always thus—
Not many years have passed since died his wife—

**XIMENES**
Is she then dead! Eliza's dead—

**RINALDO**
She passed.
Though prayers from many a heart ascended up.
To God's high throne, still death has spared her not—
I saw her carried to the grave—no eye
Was tearless, and the poor in crowds
Prest eager for a look, a sad last look
Of her who nourished them,—

**XIMENES**
But Francesco—

**RINALDO**
Francesco! who's Francesco?

**XIMENES**
Saidst thou not
Francesco was the wretched mourner's name?

**RINALDO**
You are mistaken, he is called Gustavus—
He stood as 'twere of consciousness bereft
Intently gazing on the lifeless form—
But when at last he heard the falling earth
With hollow sound upon the coffin lid,
He then exclaimed—O God, thy worst is done I
And drawing forth a poniard from his vest
He sought to fall upon her grave and die—
His hand—so God decreed—invaded not
The sacred seat of life—unwillingly
He yielded to his son's assiduous love—
His wound was quickly healed—but not his mind
Restored to peace—for since that fatal hour
He flies the semblance of all joy, and seeks
Each various form of self-inflicted pain-
But hark! that solemn toll proclaims his hour
Of penance—wouldst thou view the mournful rites—
Behind yon jutting cliff the building stands.
I cannot be your guide—for by the shade
Of yonder tow'ring rock, the sun has passed
His noontide height, and I must hence. Farewell.

[Exit,

**XIMENES** [Alone]
Gustavus?—no; 'tis he—Francesco's self—
He cannot with his hated name put off
His fiend-like form—at sight of which my wrongs
So fiercely rush upon my wildered mind,
That vengeance chasing every meaner thought
Fires my impatient soul.—But hark! again
That brazen tone comes rolling o'er the breeze—
He is devout—devout!—religious fool!
To think that tears can wash such guilt away—
I will behold him fondly bow, and kiss
His rosary, and see how weak's this man
Who once with bold unfeeling hardihood
Of life's best treasure robbed his foolish friend.

SCENE II

Almoraddins Garden.

Enter **XIMENES**.

**XIMENES**
Yet all goes well—they know Orlando not.
Can then this monkish garb disguise me so
That e'en Gustavus knows his friend no more?—
His friend!—aye once his fondly doating friend—
Though now perchance forgotten—or if still
Remembered—if the thought of all my wrongs
Alarm him still—with consciousness of guilt
He but the more bewails the death of her—
Whose image stampt upon his writhing heart
Feeding his anguish with the constant thought
That she is lost—for ever lost—must rack
His soul with pangs more fierce than fiends invent
For those, whom heaven abandons to their care—
This, this might satisfy my burning hate
Had not Eliza's death riven my heart.
And crushed the only hope that lingered there.—
For who once loving her could think aught else
Worthy of love or worthy of desire?
Beside the rose all other flow'rets hang
Their humble heads, so other beauties droop'd
Where'er Eliza came.—But, oh! how far
Was every grace that floated round her form.

Bloom'd on her cheek or sparkled in her eye—
How far were these below the gentler charm,
That check'd my angry words ere passion spoke,
And melted me to tears, whene'er she sooth'd
The orphan's sigh or suffering peasant's groan—
And is she lost—for ever lost to me!—
Yet he still lives—yes; lives—but 'tis to know
Orlando's vengeance does not always sleep—
On this then let me dwell—the thought is balm—
His son's in love.—When woman is concern'd
'Twill be an easy task to work him harm.—
But I shall need assistance—I have mark'd.
Among the captives here, a comrade's face—
But he remembers not his early friend—
Dogs know and kiss, tho' years have laps'd, the hand
That does but little more than strike its slaves—
While man—but what of man?—I need his aid—
This solemn silence in the deaden'd air
Now broken only by the gutt'ral song
Of yonder mournful bird, should mark the hour
At which I oft have met with him I seek—
And to my wishes, lo! this way he comes.—

[Enter **RINALDO**.

Why ever thus, my son, court solitude?
For ever roaming midst these groves thou'rt seen.
While gayest sports and games engage the rest—
Does melancholy lead thee thus to seek
The solitary grove or sultry beach?
Hast thou perchance some deep, some secret woe.
To brood o'er which may sooth thy sorrow'd soul?
Or hast thou in the halls of Venice left
Some lovely mistress, who in bondage held
Thy vanquished heart, ere yet thy cruel fates
Condemn'd thee captive to these sterner foes?
My office here is comfort to bestow.—
If then in aught I can relieve thy grief.
Impart thy wish, nor doubt my friendly zeal.

**RINALDO**
Nor grief nor melancholy cause my flight
From scenes to which my thoughtless comrades haste—
Low pleasures may allay a common grief.
But what can give repose to pangs like mine—
The pangs of hopeless love?

**XIMENES**

Venetian dames
Have eyes that well may give so deep a wound.—

**RINALDO**
No, father, no—'twas not in Italy—
But here I met the spoiler of my peace—
I seek these groves, because I here have watched
Her light and airy step; and when her prayers
Have gain'd a respite to the captives' toil.
Here have I seen her smiling on their joys,
As nature smiles upon her varied works.
When from the waves the glorious sun bursts forth
To renovate and cheer the peopled earth.

**XIMENES** [Aside]
Now are the fates propitious—here's a tool
Most fit to work with—

**RINALDO**
None but the fair Euphemia's virgin charms
Could cause this love, to me more dear than life;
For as the moon's pale light, which naught revives.
Still softens all the roughness of the scene.
And gilds the craggy steep and falling wave:
So though my hopeless love consumes my heart,
Yet, still it charms and makes the future glow
So bright in fair imagination's dreams,
That moments of such bliss more than repay
The pangs I feel when reason holds the rule.

**XIMENES**
But can a brave Venetian be content
With gazing?—a Venetian once the pride
Of every gay Ridotto—can the bold
The famed Rinaldo tamely shrink and fear
A stern repulse from an unpolished girl,
Unskill'd to practise European wiles?

**RINALDO**
Dost thou then know me?—I supposed my form
So changed, that none could know Rinaldo thus.—

**XIMENES**
Know thee!—was Count Orlando known to thee?

**RINALDO**
He was my friend, and well I lov'd him too—
Fearless of danger he preserv'd my life.

Averting from my head th' uplifted axe,—

**XIMENES**
If on thy secrecy he might rely
Thou here perchance mightst recognize thy friend.—

**RINALDO**
The Count Orlando would not doubt my faith—

**XIMENES**
Then come, Rinaldo, to a friend's embrace;
For such an interview I long have sought
In this disguise—but now I find thee true.—

**RINALDO**
My friend, my friend! do we then meet again?
But oh! how chang'd!—a priest!—what means this cowl?

**XIMENES**
I wear it only for concealment's sake;
But may I hope that nothing shall escape?
Shall all I say be buried in thy breast,
Thence to be drawn but by myself alone?

**RINALDO**
Thou mayst—

**XIMENES**
Then swear by him who sav'd thy soul—

**RINALDO**
If oaths alone can win thy confidence
I ask it not—

**XIMENES**
I've wrong'd thee—pardon me—
But frequent treachery has stung my soul
So deeply, that I well may doubt if faith
Be still an inmate in the human breast,—

**RINALDO**
Hast thou then too been wounded by deceit?
I heard that dissipation's glittering tide
Was quickly sweeping all thy wealth away.—

**XIMENES**
Must I then once again call up afresh
Sorrows past cure?—My memory alone.

Ere my lips speak, renews my heart's anguish
And maddens every thought, till I avoid
With anxious care the very name of her
Who wrought my woe; and in oblivion try
To drown all traces of my wretched lot—
Vainly I thought that time with lenient hand
Would mitigate my grief's severer pangs—
But still with ago its poison seems to spread.
When first we met in Florence, lively youth
And buoyant hope spread o'er my future years
Such brilliant hues, as if the magic wand
Of old dames elf had been at pleasant work—
My heart then opened to the sun of love.
As the soft hare-bell, when Aurora's tints
Glow in the east, expands its silken leaves
To the life-giving orb.—The maid I lov'd
Was then the pride of Florence, and excell'd
In every grace, each rival's lessen'd charms—
But why so fondly dwell upon the theme?
She is not mine—the thought disturbs my brain—
It burns with all the phrensy of despair.—

**RINALDO**
Tis needless to repeat how fair she was;
I have beheld her, and have witness'd too
The general homage render'd to her charms.—

**XIMENES**
Mine was a blissful dream— for she receiv'd
Her lover with such smiles, that I believ'd
The pleasure they bestow'd could flow alone
From smiles by love inspir'd. When madly I
To her and to her father introduc'd
The viper that has stung the thoughtless fool
Who fondly cherish'd it,—It was Gustavus,
He whom thou seest playing the bigot here.—
Working on my open heart—I introduc'd
This villain to her house—for he promis'd
To guard my interests—to shield my love—
When I could not appear, to sue for me.—
In fine, he was my friend—my other half
Pleading for me.—But, liar! he betray'd me—
Invented tales, which with malignant joy
He whisper'd to her unsuspecting ear.
And taught her to believe that I was false.—
Think with what anguish, with what deadly rage
My soul was tortur'd,—Francesco stole her—
Oh! then, indeed, I knew what anguish was.—

**RINALDO**

But stop, I will await some fitter time.

**XIMENES**

Nay! this was not enough—my father—aye.
My father stretching his weak hands to stop
The miscreant in his flight, was slain by him—
Francesco slew him—with repeated blows
Struck that corpse which in death still held this wretch
For me.—
I will not think of this—depriv'd of all
Which bound me to the world, I stood awhile
As blighted and insensible to all—
But my heart beat again.—Revenge! revenge!
Exulting leapt into the throne of love
And by its very glance destroyed the boy
Who once reigned despot, where now sits this fiend.—
It spurr'd me on—urg'd me from place to place
In search of those who from my wrath had fled.—
At last I have discover'd him here retir'd
To penance—I will lay by him, and here
Will live a vampire on his son and him.
Sucking in living drops his very blood.—
Eliza—but she's dead—she's dead—I know—
I know not now how many are the years,
I've sought this man.—Thro' every clime I've bjeen—
But he is found—and hope begins to dawn
On me, as on the sailor worn with toil,
If the dark clouds should for a moment part,
And leave a glimmering of the northern star
To pierce the stormy dark abyss of night.
And guide his way—
If on thine aid, as shall occasion ask,
I might rely, my hopes were doubly sure.—

**RINALDO**

Unfold thy plans, thou'lt find in me a friend
Most willing to exert his utmost power
In aid of aught that may advance thy aim.

**XIMENES**

On this I found my plan—Anselmo loves,
As well methinks thou know'st, thine own Euphemia—

**RINALDO**

Yes, he's my rival; and their mutual love
With jealous eye and goading envy viewed

May be to thee a pledge of willing aid.

**XIMENES**
I see Gustavus harrowed by remorse
Seeks absolution by the strictest rites
Our church ordains. The maid lov'd by his son
Is taught to scoff at Christ—thence I'll work on him
To thwart their loves, while, by that passion urged
To which the sternest and the wisest vield,
Anselmo shall resist his father's will—
I know no pang wherewith to rack the heart
Like son's ingratitude and baffled love.

**RINALDO**
But how can I in aught assist thy plan?

**XIMENES**
Do thou but with Euphemia urge thy suit.
I on Anselmo's side will loose the bonds.
Whilst thou divid'st her thought with love for thee.

**RINALDO**
But canst thou think she will so soon forget—

**XIMENES**
Oh, women's hearts are easily lost and won—
Euphemia loves Anselmo now—thou next
'Mayst all her soul engage and be to her
The object of her sighs—Rinaldo's name
Sounds quite as well in sonnets or in songs—
Thy limbs are turned as well; and these and wealth
Are all they seek--
'Tis not by age they'd measure love—oh no!
With every change of seasons they would win
Some doating fool, who for a moment pleases,
And then is like a bauble thrown aside.—
Oh, leave this folly, Rinaldo! to despair!
Let's think how I may gain approach to him
Who hopes, wrapt in seclusion, none may see
The hideous devil lurking in his breast.

**RINALDO**
Here also fortune seems to favour thee.
For know, his confessor is one of those
Who fled the fate your discords often bring
On those whose turn it is to prove too weak;
And as he in thy native Florence dwelt.
The Count Orlando's name must sure have reached

This monk; and thou wilt find, I make no doubt.
The way to win an entrance through his means—
But see, my fellow captives come this way—
If thou wilt come with me we'll seek some spot
E'en more retired, and talk still more of this.

**XIMENES**
I thank thee, friend, but I have long been
To solitude, and this sad picturing used
Even to thee of all the grief I've borne
Has raised the demon here—farewell; 'twill pass.
And then again we'll meet; till then, farewell!

ACT II

SCENE I

A Hermit's Cell

Enter **XIMENES** and **DOMINIC**.

**DOMINIC**
Vicissitudes of life, how great, how strange,
Must o'er your head have passed; for when I left
Those shores, which oft by flattering fancy raised
Before my sleepless sight, have caused the tears
Of sweet remembrance to bedew my cheek;
Then was thy name for riches, power, for all
In fine, that weak-eyed mortals can desire
In every mouth.—Thy name was bandied round
As 'twere a proverbed truth; but now a cowl
Invests the head where shone the richest gems
The east or west could give.—Thy scanty robes
Scarce shelter from the blast the form that once
With gold and purple decked, seemed still as dressed
Below its seeming.— E'en thy name is changed.

**XIMENES**
Aye, father, when I first was known to thee.
My heart felt deep the love of worldly pomp;
I thought that man was born for glittering vests,
For all that gaudy show, by which the proud
Would fain conceal the rotten nothingness
On which their frail mortality depends.
But God, though not by one o'erwhelming blow,
Has weaned my heart from all these earthly cares.

**DOMINIC**

But how did God thus change thy dangerous state?
Did he despoil thee of thy wealth alone?
Or did he other deeper wounds inflict
Upon thy heart? When I was last in Florence
I heard thou wert to wed fair Bianchi's child,
And all around seemed smiling on thy suit.

**XIMENES**

Aye, there was the curing sting—I lost her—
I need not tell thee how—women are frail—
Suffice to say Gustavus was the fiend
That hung enchanting round his friend to snare
This Eve.—My love for both soon changed to hatred—
I gamed—I plunged into the gulph of vice
In search of peace; but no such peace was there.
At last, for still religion had not lost
All influence, I went to Holy Land,
And there I knelt upon the sepulchre.
I know not what I felt—it seemed a spark
Of grace was granted to my guilty soul
Among the rest—for shame so strong of thoughts
Which day and night I'd harboured in my breast
Against my foes, seized on my mind, that all
My wayward thoughts of vanity were gone;

**DOMINIC**

Great cause indeed hast thou to bless thy God
That he has made thee feel how mad is man.
Who himself guilty dares to punish guilt.
While many die, nor know that this vain world
Is the deceit of a poor passing show.
Where tended next thy steps; and what has brought
Thee to this isle?

**XIMENES**
Upon the tomb I vowed
My life to universal good.—The years
That since have glided o'er my head, have seen
The servant of his God upon the coast
Of Africa; and there his labours have been blessed
With many a convert; but while thus engaged
Among these savages, my thought would turn
To this Gustavus.—Oft I fancied sounds
That urged me to discover his retreat,
And seek to bring him to a state more fit
For God's pure grace to work upon. Five years

I now have passed exploring various lands;
At last, arrived upon this isle, I find
That here he dwells, and that by thee confessed,
He humbly takes thy guidance on the way
That leads the pardoned penitent to heaven.
In thee an ancient friend I meet, and since
To holy hands like thine the trust is given,
I will again away to distant shores,
Where other labours still my presence claim.

**DOMINIC**
Not so, my son; for God has been thy guide.
Know that although Gustavus spends his days
In penance and in grief, he never yet
Has sought remission from our holy church.

**XIMENES**
'Tis strange! for surely his repentance seems
To weigh his spirit down—

**DOMINIC**
Whene'er I urge
The duty of confession, wildly starting
He leaves me, or with horror trembling, cries
That God could never hearken to his prayers,
Since he regrets not his committed sins
But for the sake of her, who shared his guilt,
He reeks not aught that may befall himself.

**XIMENES**
Could but my humble efforts work this change
So much desired, I should be blessed indeed.

**DOMINIC**
Thy opportune arrival augurs well;
For I am often called to distant parts.
Where by the dying captive's lonely couch
With sacred rites I sooth the parting soul.—
On such an errand to the other coast
At early morn I'm summoned to repair.—
Gustavus always bears my absence ill.
For he dislikes my brethren, nor has yet
Permitted any to approach his cell.
If thou wilt share my dwelling, I may hope
To introduce thee to his knowledge soon.

**XIMENES**
This must not be; for should he learn my name

I fear some rash and impious attempt
Upon himself. Let me remain unknown.
Save as a pilgrim of his native land
Returning from the sepulchre of Christ.

**DOMINIC**
'Tis well; and when I visit him this eve.
As such I will announce thee; thou, meanwhile.
Art welcome to my cell and humble fare,

**XIMENES**
I take thy offered kindness, and will here.
At least while thou'rt away, and if thou thinkest
My weak endeavours may in aught avail
To gain this sinner o'er to grace, command
God's willing slave—I will await thee here.

[Exeunt.


SCENE II

Almoraddin's Garden.

Enter **ALMORADDIN** and **ANSELMO**.

**ALMORADDIN**
If to thy view my heart could but disclose
What on its inmost core inscribed it bears,
Thou'dst see thy name so with Euphemia's joined,
So mixed and linked, it would be hard to say
Which there held mastery.
As pilgrim o'er the sandy Syrian plain
Reclines fatigued, when first he meets the shade
Of some fair grove whence he may view his home.
And though his heart beats high with anxious hope
That he shall see those scenes, which raised by fancy.
Cheered his lone path, still fearing clings to whence
He first may view his lowly native roof.
Lest he in dull reality should lose
Those happy visions of his richer mind—
So I the drear desert of this short life
At length passed o'er, in sight of that last spot
Where weary nature rests, upon my child
In heartfelt peace reposed—her life thou'st saved
Thou stood'st before so near my heart, methought
I could not feel more love for mine own son;
But now it seems as if the love I bear

My child, engrafted stood on yours—if aught
Thou will'st my power may grant, when named, 'tis thine.

**ANSELMO**
What can a son of a kind father ask!
And hast thou not a father's care and love
Extended from my childhood to my youth!

**ALMORADDIN**
What I have done by love of merit urged
I willing did—thy virtue was the cause—
I was but God's mean instrument to give
What he decreed should here be thy reward.—
If thy desires by high ambition swayed,
Should point perchance to thy aspiring sight
Fame's glittering bauble, I shall smooth the way—
My noble friends shall to the sultan's smile
Soon clear the arduous path for thy approach.
If luxury before thine eyes hath spread
Her envied gifts, and all thou want'st is gold.
My riches shall supply thy want.

**ANSELMO**
Ne'er did ambition's spark lurk in my breast.
Nor wish for luxury disturb my peace.
I nought desire—but yes—one sighed-for wish—
Oft with the fondest love, thou'dst call me son.
Long has the smothered flame within my heart
From mine own view been hidden—I know not him
Who could withstand those more than magic charms;
If but a moment she should smiling look
On the poor wanderer as his way he wends.
He should in vain attempt to move his feet,
But fascinated, as the travellers tell
Are Indian birds by serpents' magic eye,
Bound to the spot by viewless chains he'd stand—
And I who've watched the beauties of her face
Like spring's first rose, each day some nascent charm
Displaying to my view.—Could I be blest
With her sweet smiles, and still remain unmoved?

**ALMORADDIN**
All that my cherished hopes e'er plann'd
Has rested on thy union with my child.
But she Mahomet prophet deems of God—
Thou Christ, as son of him who reigns in heaven.
Oft in imagination's dreams I've seen
The happiest prospects painted to my view,

Where thou with love's fair bonds to her wert joined;
When sudden like some envious demon's touch,
This thought would change the imaged bliss to grief.

## ANSELMO

Do not thus rend from my poor heart that love
Which, as the flowering shrub gives to the soil
O'er which it spreads all beauty and all w orth.
Has caused whate'er thou mayst esteem in me.
If from my breast thou tear all love of her,
Thou'lt leave me but the hope that Azrael
Will cut my thread, and kindly thus allow
My poor rent heart a refuge in the grave.
But no—still, still may love unite us both—
She may adore Mahomet—I my Christ.

## ALMORADDIN

My son, deceive not with false hopes thy heart;
I cannot risk the safety of my child;
Mahomet has his choicest blessings show er'd
Upon my head, and shall I prove the cause
Euphemia leave his worship and forget
Him, who her father's happiness has caused;
For soon yielding to love for thee, she'll bow
Obedient to thy laws; for oft the heart.
Which like the oak unbent by stormy wind
Undaunted could resist gainst threats, will bow
Like the weak ozier, fore a softer breath.

## ANSELMO

Destroy not by one word the cherished hope
Which, as the sun when from the purpling wave
Its car effulgent issues to the world
Gilds to the traveller's eye with splendid ray
The distant mount, the wide sandy desert.
And the vast stormy main; alone has gilt
Futurity to me,—But well I know
Thy speech is empty—thus thou wouldst repay
With fair promises, and when glitt'ring words
Have softly soothing issued from thy mouth.
Thou think'st all debts are with thy words discharged.

## ALMORADDIN

Hast thou then had no proof of love from me?
Must I to thy remembrance bring how I
With tenderest care fostered thy childhood once?
And did not I, for thee, when fortune frowned
Malignant o'er thy father's best laid plans.

Did not I raise him up from indigence?
Did not I save him from the grasp of one,
Who proud with new gained power would tread him down?
But one way still remains, confess but this,
That Mecca holds great Allah's chosen slave,
And she is thine—

**ANSELMO**
I see!—'tis all in vain;
Thou wouldst but colour thy denial thus.
Thou canst not hope that I'd abjure my God.

**ALMORADDIN**
And yet thou think'st that I should thus expose
Euphemia to abjure Mahomet's power,
For well thou know'st she could not long resist.

**ANSELMO**
Mahomet—but—

**ALMORADDIN**
Speak not to me of him
With slighting speech; remember, he to us
Is like thy Christ, and joined like him to God.

**ANSELMO**
This is too thin a veil for thy intent;
I am mayhap not rich enough for thee.

**ALMORADDIN**
Stop! let me hear no more; thou dost forget
O'ercome by passion, both thyself and me.

[Exit,

**ANSELMO**
My friend! Nay 'tis too late— he's gone in anger.
And could I then him, who my friend has proved,
When all around in darkness seemed absorpt,
Could I brand him with falseness, and insult
Him with that blackest charge, ingratitude?
Eupliemia! fairest flower of these fair isles!
Shall then another pluck and wear thy love
Enshrined within his heart? Shall I alone
No longer feel the power of those sweet smiles.
On softest coral lip so softly playing?
Shall that fair breast no longer anxious heave.
As oft I've seen it heave with care for me.

But occupied with love for others, feel
For me, as I were but a stranger there?
One way I still have left—Mahomet's power—
What, could I harbour such a thought?
My Saviour!—I abjure my God, who came
Not rayed in splendor to redeem mankind.
But suffered all that demons could inflict.
To save his dear lost race, who bore unmoved
Whate'er his foes, whate'er ungrateful man
Of foulest insult on his head could heap—
Shall he find me ungrateful too like them?
Must I then yield all hope? God cannot wish
To separate what's joined by heaven-born bonds?
But why with hope's illusions feed my love?
'Tis e'en too true; alas! to me she's lost.

[He stands aside wrapt in thought

[Enter **EUPHEMIA**.

**EUPHEMIA**
I wonder where Anselmo hides himself;
He used not late to treat Eupheinia thus,
But waiting on my steps, he'd cheer my hours
With softest converse on his purest love.
Perchance he would not hear the grateful thanks
My heart would speak for her whose life he saved—
Ah! there he stands.—How my poor heart is beating.
He's wrapt in thought—perchance he thinks on me.

[She approaches, puts a crown of roses on his head, which he tears unconsciously.

**ANSELMO**
Away!—begone!—

**EUPHEMIA**
Why thus, Anselmo? what, thou tear the rose!
Contemnest thou then her gift, whose life thou sayedst;
Or dost thou love me not?—not even speak
To thy Eupheinia! Nay, thou canst not thus.
Oft hast thou said my smiles a tyger's rage
Could quell; thou art no tyger, but my love.—
Wilt thou not heed me now? look but on me.
And if thou smilest—thy Eupheinia then—

**ANSELMO**
Euphemia mine!—tempt not my weakness thus.

**EUPHEMIA**

Yes, thine—Euphemia's thine—is it not so?

**ANSELMO**

Away! away!—leave me, I prithee do.

**EUPHEMIA**

Then misery's my lot indeed, if truth
Finds not, Anselmo! in thy breast a place;
Where can I hope to find its blessed seat?
Euphemia asks—tell me what unknown fault—
Make me thy very slave, but frown not on me.

**ANSELMO**

My love!—but why thus call thee now? thou art
No longer his, whose life hung on those words,
Euphemia's mine. All happiness is flown
With the fond hope that hand might once be mine.

**EUPHEMIA**

And what can hinder, that thou shouldst obtain
What is already thine? If women's oaths
Are registered in heaven, I swear by all
That Moslems sacred hold, by Mecca's tomb.
That none if thou dost not, shall e'er obtain
From me, while life remains, this virgin hand.

**ANSELMO**

Do I then hear aright? My love! My all!
Hear, hear O heaven her vow, and join with hers
My own; for by the holy rood I swear
None shall divide me from Euphemia's love.—
Do I but dream? repeat once more those words,
Say once again, thou lov'st.

**EUPHEMIA**

As midst the dark and troubled waves, the rock
Rears high unmoved its head, so shall my love
Through life's dread storms remain unchanged-
Thou know'st not sure how weak is woman's breast,
Or thou wouldst not by doubting rend it thus.—

**ANSELMO**

I knew not what I did; for stung by thoughts
That maddening sunk within my breaking heart,
I spoke unconscious words. But why that crown?

**EUPHEMIA**

I was to lead thee crowned as king of sports
My father gives in honour of thyself,—
But see, the pilgrim comes; I must away
Another garland to prepare. Adieu.

[Exit.

[Enter **XIMENES**.

**XIMENES**
For ever with these infidels thou'rt seen.
Who daily curse our Saviour's holy name.

**ANSELMO**
Bade not our Saviour man to be at peace
With all? Shewed not he pity unto all?

**XIMENES**
Yes, but he meant by that, not friendly love:
Not that thou shouldst vouchsafe to them, what love
Alone may give to friends and dearer ties.

**ANSELMO**
It ill becomes thy holy badge to fan
With hollow sounding words the spark of discord.

**XIMENES**
Patience! my soul; thank God that I am used
To meet abuse where I intend to serve.
I am not moved by laughers or by boys,
Who think it wit to scoff religion's sway;
Though all like thee my righteous zeal oppose
And scorn, unmoved I'd execute my trust;
But much I fear religion's seed has found
A soil most barren in thy hardened heart—
Did not I see a Moslam syren here
With smiles and witchery luring thee to ruin?

**ANSELMO**
Arouse not, priest, my indignation—stop,
Whilayet thou may'st, that cursed lying tongue,
While yet my hand respects the badge thou wear'st.

**XIMENES**
I knew all this; 'tis even as I thought.
As my dear master met revilers, I
Must not complain; I shall not then omit
Whate'er my master's duty prompts -- lures not

That witching infidel with vilest arts.—

**ANSELMO**
While yet I may ere anger gains the rule
I'll hence, and fly from thy accursed snares.

[Exit.

**XIMENES**
What e'en so hot? the leaven still will work—
What is it moves me in this boy? His voice
Went to my inmost feeling— sounds like these
Once caused my heart to vibrate as they fell.
His eye, though it spoke words of anger, still
Seem'd like to hers who once in gayer times
Would speak her soul by means of them, and said
With them e'en more than with her words—she lov'd—
And love dipt in the dew of her soft eye
Would pass on beams of light through her dark lash
To me.—Oh, fool! still harping on that string?
Those eyes betrayed me!
But now to nobler deeds.—Within this hour
I meet Francesco—Yet my heart is still—
I feel no fluttering—Whence is this calm?
Is it some devil sitting on my heart
Caring this thought, uprooting all the rest?
Within an hour I breathe the very air
That plays upon the lips of this Francesco—
Oh! that mine own might still therein such poison
As would each day infect some drop of life—
But that would hurt alone his body.—No;
I would not work on that—I wish him strength
To combat with the devil I let loose.
Though ne'er to conquer it—Let him find strength
After each lash to bear another's pain—
For so I'll lash his mind—'twere better death
Should seize upon him, tho' 'twere with all the pomp
Of racks and wheels, that wait on meek eyed justice.

[Exit.


ACT III

SCENE I

Gustavus' Oratory.

Enter **GUSTAVUS**.

**GUSTAVUS**
It must be so—My guilt revealed at death
To her whom I had wronged, has made her curse me—
Else why for years this weight upon my mind?
A mother weeps her son but for a time—
And time dries all the widow's tears—prisoners
They say at last have lov'd their hideous caves,
And when released have left them as their home,
Yet I am fill'd with thoughts from which I fly
To bodily inflictions—as if pain
Could equal grief.— I would ere now have sought
Rest from despairing love in other worlds;
But then the thought of meeting there the two
Whom I have wronged, startles my soul with shame.
And paints the future state with darker shades
Than e'en the present wears—though these are black.
I feed, I breathe, 1 sleep on grief—no time
Of rest—a moment's calm may sometimes pass,
Such as deceives the novice on the sea,
But warns the sailor of the rising storm.
Last night I lay reclined on yonder cliff,
And sought oblivion gazing on the sun—
Its blood red disk was setting in the west,
And all the clouds, the heavens, the sea were clothed
In vest of crimson light.— The air was still—
No cloud was moving—no green wave was breaking;
The distant cliffs of ancient Greece were lost
In the red coloured air, and the few rocks.
That nearer rear'd their heads, seem'd rapt in sleep—
Hardly on their tall heads the sun's light played
And there it seem'd like the white hair'd glisten
On old man's head.— This nature's stillness seized
At length on me, and quelled awhile my groans—
Sleep's balmy hand soon lock'd my senses fast—
When from this corse my soul appear'd to scape,
And big with joy fly basking to the sun,
As if it had forgot this earth and grief—
I felt as if I entered into all.
Though yet identical.— My vision seemed
To reach farther than the sun's ray, and pierc'd
What sent them hack.— My quickened hearing caught
The sounds of the most distant volving spheres,
Mingling in harmony.— I gambol'd proudly
In the bright sevenfold rays—for it appeared
As if they sought to mingle with the beam

Of Godhead forming me—far beyond reach
Of cloud or mortal gaze, my flight was flown.—
This planet seemed already less to sight
Than does Diana's shield.—Dimly were seen
The earth and ocean's boundary; the one
Like an expanded sheet of burnished gold
Shone clear, the other with no splendor bright
Seem'd yet of that same work only unpolished.
I soon arrived 'midst beings like myself;
And scarcely had I cast a glance around
When she, who once with a kind sister's care,
In honour's path had cheer'd and truly lov'd me.—
But, now—oh! no! she cannot curse, though fallen,
Her brother still must to her heart be dear.
She hail'd me, saying, "One awaits thee here,
Whose happiness e'en here imperfect seems;
For as each night permits these souls to seek
The earth, she always tends unto one spot,
And there hangs listening to thy grief—apart
From these, she spends her solitary hours—
Come then with me to cheer her solitude."
This said, we flew.— But soon I saw a spectre
Emerging from the sun—It was Orlando,
Treading the space with immaterial foot,
Like the pale lightning on my sight he flashed,
But passed not like it—for unmoved he stood
Laughing in scorn, not loud but deep—then cried,
With voice that drown'd all music of the spheres.
Vain is thy search! To thee Eliza's lost!
I am thy partner! Hell thy bridal bed!
I am thy fiend, and stand by thee for ever!"
Here I awoke, and found that darker night
Had stretched its huge thick mantle o'er the scene,
That thus had given the semblance of a calm.—
But well known steps strike on my listening ear;
This must be Dominic—

[Enter **DOMINIC**.

Good father, hail!

**DOMINIC**
Son, I am come to tell thee I must hence
To visit one, whose tardy penitence
By sudden stroke of death but now called forth,
Yet hopes to fray his weed-choaked way to heaven.
I may be absent long; for he, perchance.
Some days may linger.

**GUSTAVUS**

This afflicts me;
For, save from thee, I know not where to seek
Counsel and aid; and though thou canst not give
The strength I need, still will thy friendly words
Steal me at times e'en from myself. Where now
To look for spiritual guidance—where
For one to give my alms amongst the poor,
Or to direct my steps in penitence?

**DOMINIC**

These calls, my son, I cannot but obey;
Yet even, when thus summon'd, I deplore
Thy lonely state, and grieve that I must quit thee.
But now there is come one whom I have known
From infancy; who occupied for long
Amid the Afric deserts, late has left
The Holy Land; a man of special grace,
And one who seems to tread the slippery path
That guides to heaven, with foot most firm and sure—
His age now renders him less apt for toils
And dangers like to those gone through.—Untired,
However, in the work grateful to God,
He seeks somewhere to rest, but not neglect
His duty's call. Hither with me he's come;
And may I hope thou wilt receive him well?
For he will prove to thee a most true guide.

**GUSTAVUS**

He may; but still he will not wear that form
To which my eyes have so familiar grown;
They seem to lack their food when thou'rt not here.
He will not have thy voice, to which I bow
As 'twere by instinct, nor will he put forth
The kindness thou hast used towards me.—A friend
Is formed by time; friendship's of tardy growth—
As no new shrub supplies the lofty oak
Which gave us shade, so can no stranger's care
Afford the ease thou giv'st unto our pains.

**DOMINIC**

Think not that I abandon thee, my son!
When I'm away—thou still wilt want a guide.
'Tis better that in him thou shouldst confide;
He is at hand—say, wilt thou see him?

**GUSTAVUS**

Well,
As thou think'st fit; I'm all resigned in thee.
In thee I put my trust.

**DOMINIC** [Goes out and returns with **XIMENES**]
Behold, my son, my friend, the holy man.
Father Ximenes, to whose pious care
I would commit the saving of thy soul—

**XIMENES**
God bless thee, son, and may he grant to thee
Whate'er of worldly pains or gifts he knows
Most fit to take thee from the claws of him
Who roars in quest of prey to feed his lust.

**GUSTAVUS**
Amen to this thy blessing; and thank thee;
For if the heavenly word be truly spoken.
Prayers have avail, and thine will bring their fruit.

**DOMINIC**
Well then, my son!—farewell; I leave thee here
In hands to which I hope the grace is given
To lead thee up to heaven. I must away
This eve, and much is yet undone.—Farewell;
And may a blessing fall, while I'm away.
Upon thy head.

**GUSTAVUS**
What, then, so soon I lose
My friend! But if it is God's will, farewell.
Remember me in the orisons sent
Each day to heaven.

**DOMINIC**
I will, you need not doubt.
Farewell.

[Exit.

**GUSTAVUS**
I thank my holy father, under God,
That he has given me one with worth like thine;
From him I learn that thou hast visited
The spot where God suffered.—Oh, would that I
Had grace to go unto that spot where fell
His blood to cleanse the earth. But I'm unworthy;
God has struck down my strength; I can do nothing,

Save groan and weep, and that is vain.

**XIMENES**
Oh, no!
Tears washed the thief of all his heinous crimes,
And shall not thine avail? and though 'tis true
We must esteem the sight of Holy Land
A grant from heaven's self; still tears are gifts
From that same place, and show that heaven receives
The grief as some atonement for the sin.

**GUSTAVUS**
I should not thus despair;—yet gazing hence
Whither my sins have hurl'd me, up to heav'n
I so despond, desponding is despair.—

**XIMENES**
Oh, weakness worthy of an infidel.
But not of thee.—What sin, save that of Judas
Betraying under friendly show a friend.
Is upon record, as unpardon'd?—True
That wrought despair.

**GUSTAVUS**
Oh! 'tis too true, I am cursed;
My sins drags me to hell—it is decreed—

**XIMENES**
What is this madness by thy words implied;
This is to tempt thy God—from which 'tis said
Thou shouldst forbear—

**GUSTAVUS**
Yes, it is easy thus to say.
Forbear.—But, oh! if thou hadst lost that jewel
I have thus lost— for ever—mind, for ever,
Thou wouldst, couldst not be calm.

**XIMENES**
Too well I know
Thy loss,— Thou'st lost heaven's best gift -- a wife—
But still thou mayst obtain her sight in heav'n.

**GUSTAVUS**
Oh, no! for me there is no hope—no heav'n.

**XIMENES**
I know not what to understand—no heaven!

No hope!—Oh, yes; there is a hope for all;
God's word is given unto all, all sinners.

**GUSTAVUS**
'Tis true; but not to such as me— thou'st said
Judas was left, and so am I—But hold,
I can no more—my mind is rack'd with thought.
Thou must have felt on Afric's burning sands
The hot Sirocco's force—but that can give
No image of my thoughts.— They sap the strength
From all my bones.— They heat my very brain.
And stifle in my breast all breath of joy.
But tell me, thou hast been in Holy Land,
How fare the Christians there, 'midst such rank weeds
Of Paganism? Ho they yet keep their souls
in faith's well burnished armour, or pollute
Their sacred creed with some unholy rites;
Or do they mingle with their creed some forms
Of other faiths!

**XIMENES** [Aside]
He thinks to fly the spur
I doubt who now excel, Pagans or us;
For in all countries, where my steps I turn,
I find our simple dogmas warped to uses,
God ne'er thought of.— Such superstitious forms
Are now observed, that all the crowd bewitched
Employ the holiest words to call up devils.
And seek their fates upon the turning leaf.

**GUSTAVUS**
But this alone pervades the lowest dregs;
It has not yet ascended to the noble,
Or to the learned.

**XIMENES**
Yes, even to them;
For amongst others I could tell; let this
Suffice. When first I reached the sacred city
I went unto the sepulchre.— 'Twas night;
The glimmering flames flickered on the torch's wick,
And their red light waving with the loud wind,
Threw something holy on the spot, as glanced
The light on columns and on blackened walls.
There was no sound on earth, saving the awful breath
Arising from the stirring air which mocked
The deep full tones giv'n by the organ's swell
In pillar'd minster.—Prostrate yet in prayer,

I saw two forms advance—the dark glow
Thrown o'er their anxious face, seemed as it were
To raise them above men.—The one, who seemed
By his pale cheek and sunken eye, near death.
Could hardly hold himself; the other drest
In garbs of holy use supported him.
While round their feet he formed a circling fence
Upon the hallowed spot, on which our Lord,
From death awakening triumphed o'er the grave.
By adjurations deep calling on him
Who had inspired the traitor of our God,
They forced a demon up; howling with pain
He came all hideous.—Well assured that none.
Save those who gave themselves, were in his power,
I tied not—and o'erheard his dreadful words—
He said, Thy wish is granted, hell awarded
Before thou asked.—But of thy foe's perdition
Thy soul must pay the price."—The maniac cried,
I care not—take my soul!—to see his pain.
Will ease the torments you may heap on me"—
This said, retiring from the sepulchre
He fell and died.

**GUSTAVUS**
But was this man of rank?

**XIMENES**
Aye, so they said—Orlando Count;
I can't remember of what place.

**GUSTAVUS**
Orlando!
Say you Orlando? Oh! all cry me damned;
And I've deserved it.

**XIMENES**
What thou! wast thou—

**GUSTAVUS**
Oh! what said I!—Oh, heaven, thy hand is heavy;
How can I hope?

**XIMENES**
Thou canst the words of God.

**GUSTAVUS**
I am condemned alike by heav'n and hell,

**XIMENES**

I do not understand thy words, they seem
To say what I cannot, would not believe.

**GUSTAVUS**

Oh! go now, and leave me to myself, go hence,
I will converse with thee when more at rest.
There need no words—farewell.

**XIMENES**

Well, even so;
I am but God's mean slave, and act alone
For him; till thy commands shall call, farewell.

[Exeunt,


SCENE II

A Room in Gustavus's houses

Enter **ALMORADDIN**.

The Iman says, a pilgrimage to Mecca made
Will purify such marriage from all sin;
Yet must I fear that my severer friend,
Firm in observance of his stricter faith,
Will sternly interpose, nor let his son
Expect a father's sanction to his love,
But lo! he comes.

[Enter **GUSTAVUS**.

My steps are hither bound
On business of weight— I come to talk
About thy son.— Thou knowest my daughter's life
Was saved by him.

**GUSTAVUS**

Thou art the first from whom
I learn the news so welcome to my heart.

**ALMORADDIN**

Hast thou alone not heard, that while this morn,
Along the western coast myself and child
Were sailing o'er the softly swelling waves,
A gale o'ertook our vessel in its way—

The sails yet flying caught the tempest's force;
And soon the lofty mast, riven by the shock,
Fell and was buried in the boiling surge—
Then quick the heaving billows swept the deck,
As if, when each tumultuous wave retired.
It gained new strength.— Weary at length and spent,
We both were hurl'd into the yawning deep—
Euphemia carried by the rapid tide
Was struggling seen from shore.— Thy noble son.
Unmindful of the proudly beating storm.
Seeing but her he loved, rushed to her rescue;
With one firm hand bore up my sinking child,
The other buffetted the curling waves,
Which angry at their loss, their braving load
Dashed with impetuous fury on the strand.
Their malice overcome, he to my arms
His fainting charge consigned, as I began
To mourn my bitter loss.

**GUSTAVUS**
'Twas brave indeed.
But it ne'er reached m'y ears till now.—My soul
Could never boast of deed so nobly done.

**ALMORADDIN**
I thought not that himself would tell his fame,
But sure Ximenes might, for he the whole
Unmoved unaiding viewed.

**GUSTAVUS**
He's wrapt in thought
Intense of heavenly things, nor aught observes
That passes here.

**ALMORADDIN**
It may perchance be so
But vet I love him not; for oft is seen
That bitter smile upon his curling lip,
Which tells of thoughts deep buried in his breast.
And makes the gazer start.

**GUSTAVUS**
'Tis but his custom.—
He smiles at human folly, wasting life
On baubles light as ocean's foam, which seems
Awhile a thing of consequence, and straight
It leaves no trace upon the sea, or thought
In memory of man.

**ALMORADDIN**
I came not idly to converse of him,
Most grateful to thy son, I offered all
That he could ask—But all that I could tender.
Of jewels, wealth, or high estate refused,
He asked my daughter's hand—

**GUSTAVUS**
Euphemia's!

**ALMORADDIN**
Even so, and I refused—

**GUSTAVUS**
Thank God,
[Aside
My son
Is spared the crime of adding to my woes.

**ALMORADDIN**
My task, I see, is vain; but why refuse
Consent?

**GUSTAVUS**
Thy daughter in Mahomed's faith
Is trained—my son in Christ's.

**ALMORADDIN**
'Tis as I feared
But have we then no hope? I've heard methinks
That thy religion's head has power to grant
Such dispensation from its laws, as we
From Allah's earthly image also gain.

**GUSTAVUS**
Not in a case like this—

**ALMORADDIN**
'Twere useless here
Further to urge my suit.—I cannot ask
That thou shouldst break religion's sacred laws—
But teach me how to offer to thy son
The grateful tribute of a father's heart
For service such as his—so vast a debt
I never can repay--

**GUSTAVUS**

We owe thee much;
And, though my son has saved thy daughter's life,
'Tis but a small return for what we owe—
If I may ask a further boon; 'tis this
To let Euphemia see thy son no more—
For love by absence only can be cured—
This fails not to detect all spurious love;
A weed that shoots so like the nobler plant
That time alone its baseness can disclose.

**ALMORADDIN**
Prudence commands it and it shall be done;
But I must hence, I could not meet thy son
And see his grief while yet my heart oppressed
By its own sorrow deeply feels for his
And mourns the wayward fate, that thwarts his love.

[Exit.

**GUSTAVUS**
Methought this happiness of those I love
Could not be lasting.—Heav'n forbids such joy;
Nor lets a guilty wretch, like me, find peace
In contemplating that of all around—
Can I—with hands imbrued in blood of one.
On whose grey locks I never dare to think—
Whose withered arms then raised to check my crime
Had often to his bosom welcomed me.
E'en while I plotted ruin to his son—
Can I? Oh! no, if peace to such as me
Be given, 'tis but to make its value known,
That by such knowledge I might deeply feel
How bitter is its loss—-If God gave peace
To villains like myself, what recompence
Could virtue seek? What would deter the world
From vice? The secret pangs of conscious guilt
It sees not—therefore needs the discipline
Of outward pain.—My misery proceeds
From guilt alone.—This has perverted all
My warmest wishes and my wisest plans
To means of further punishment—But see
Anselmo comes—Grief sits upon his brow,
And with her chilling finger deeply presses
The furrows of his sorrow—I must speak—
Must urge him to comply; but weighed thus down.
How can I meet my son unconscious still
Of all my crimes?—I must, or he may live
To suffer torments such as I endure.

[Enter **ANSELMO**.

There is a load upon thy father's breast,
My dearest son, which thou hast thrown thereon.
How comes it thou hast sought a Moslam's hand?

**ANSELMO**
I never dreamt thou couldst oppose the match
With one so oft the subject of thy praise.
Whose beauty was unrivalled, and whose heart,
Thou saidst, was glowing with the noblest flame
That honour or that virtue could excite.

**GUSTAVUS**
Thou know'st not what thou sayst—dost not remember
That God the father's sins upon the child
Oft visiteth—wherefore then wilt thou increase
My load of crimes?

**ANSELMO**
Of crimes!

**GUSTAVUS**
Have I betrayed
What I so long had locked within my breast?
But it is said—I cannot now retract.—
Yes, of my crimes the load must fall on thee—
For know, thy sire's a villain—nay, much more.—
I cannot speak my crimes e'en to my son;
And God, I feel, has raised us up so high
To make our fall more terrible to both.

**ANSELMO**
But can it be in truth, my sire is guilty?
Tell me, what crimes.—

**GUSTAVUS**
It boots not now to tell—
I would retain my son. If he knew all.
He would despise and curse his father's name.—
Avoid but this new crime, and heaven perchance
To gentle pity moved, may spare a part
Of what I fear must fall upon thy head.

**ANSELMO**
Keep me no longer in suspence, but say
What crimes call down such vengeance from above.

But no!—I'll not believe—'Tis Ximenes,
Who thus has raised such fancies in thy brain.

**GUSTAVUS**
Oh! would to God, my son, it was but so:
Oh no! it is not idle fantasy
Has caused me thus to shun the haunts of men.—
Tis guilt! 'Tis guilt, I fear more foul than heaven
Can ever cleanse, tho' God should pour his blood
Upon my soul. Though first the flames of hell
Should play upon my soul, and as my crimes
Must also bring the wrath of heaven on thee.
Do not increase its power.

**ANSELMO**
But I have sworn
To wed her.

**GUSTAVUS**
Have you sworn?

**ANSELMO**
I have sworn with her
To live.

**GUSTAVUS**
Couldst thou but for a moment feel
The sting that's here so deeply fixed, no art
Can drag it hence, thou wouldst not, couldst not doubt.

**ANSELMO**
It may so chance. I'll have no need to doubt.
She may reject the son of one disgraced
By crimes so great as thou hast said are thine.

**GUSTAVUS**
And wilt thou tear the veil from thine own sire
And shew his guilty soul bare to her view?

**ANSELMO**
I would not basely now deceive Euphemia.

**GUSTAVUS**
Is then the world to know thy father's guilt?

**ANSELMO**
She never will betray Anselmo's secret.

**GUSTAVUS**

And if she hold thy chains, wilt thou not break them?

**ANSELMO**

Euphemia's chains, if she but smile, shall hold
With firmer bond her lover. If the world shall lower,
The breath of heaven in anger blast
All that we here possess, knit by such love
With firmer hearts we shall resist our griefs.

**GUSTAVUS**

Dost thou then brave the anger of thy God
Think how he may afflict. Thy sheltering arms
May wind in vain around her heaving breast.
The lightning of his pow'r, the sudden blow
May, as it were, in sportive dalliance strike.
And thou be left a withered lonely stem
In the bleak desert of this life—alone.

**ANSELMO**

Thinkst thou I can love her more when mine?
I could not even now survive her loss.
But, as a flowering shrub on some hard rock.
Soon as the rill, that washed its base, is turned.
Dies with the herb its shade had sheltered long.
So if the Almighty turned his smile of life
From her, I never could survive the loss,
But as she pined, should pine and die with her.

**GUSTAVUS**

So thought I too, when first thy mother blest
My longing heart but where can mortals hide
Their guilty heads from heaven's all piercing sight.
God forced the wretch to live, who'd lost the tie
Alone which bound him unto life. My son,
If not that I abjure thee as my son.
Forget Euphemia's love.

**ANSELMO**

Thou wouldst not wish
That I whom thou hast taught to hold my word
More dear than life, should break a plighted oath.

**GUSTAVUS**

Anselmo will—

**ANSELMO**

I must not stop! your tears

May else unman my heart when reason fails.

[Exeunt.

SCENE I

Gustavus' Anti-chamber.

**XIMENES** and **GUSTAVUS** meet.

**GUSTAVUS**
Welcome Ximenes, thy approach can quell
The storm within me to an instant calm.

**XIMENES**
What is it that disturbs thy sought-for peace?
For oft I've seen depicted on that brow
More than should meet the wondering gazer's sight:
Something most heavy weighs upon thy heart—
Declare what it may be, and I shall try
To minister to thy mind's disease.—
For as the skilful leech to hidden wound
Cannot a cure apply, until he first
Probe its depth and extent; so cannot we
Give balm or ease to mental wounds unknown.

**GUSTAVUS**
I would not tell my shame, to utter deeds
Like those that weigh me down, would blast my tongue—
But yet they hang so heavy on my heart,
I wish I could—but no! I have not power—

**XIMENES**
Oh weak man, what avails my knowledge
In balance with the knowledge of thy God! [placed
I well remember now of one like thee.
Of one who acted like thy foolish self,
Would not on the same point obey his God—
Would not confess—
He had betrayed his friend—his friend had loved—
No poet could describe her whom he loved;
Whene'er she'd walk you'd think a Dian trod,
And when she'd smile, tho' 'twas an anchorite
E'en he'd forget that all was vanity—

He won by gifts the sire for he had wealth
And brib'd all round to utter calumnies
Of Or—

**GUSTAVUS**
Orlando!

**XIMENES** [Aside]
What is this I've said—
I must beware.—Orlando sayst thou?—no—
No—that was not bis name—but thou art pale;
Does aught affect thee?

**GUSTAVUS**
No; I thought—but no—
Go on, I pray.

**XIMENES** [Aside]
Oh, then it stings!—I'll on.
And press it to the core. He basely slandered
Orontes; he it was, and while his friend
Hoped he was wooing her for him, he pour'd
Such artful tales into her listening ear,
That she, at last to fly the fancied wretch,
Cast her poor self into the traitors arms.
His joy was but short lived, for soon she died.
And he an outcast fled. I found him sick.
In a low loathsome hut of poorest slaves.
His eyes scarce turned upon my vestment's form
When sudden with a phrenzied haste he grasped
Th' apparel of his bed, to hide his face—
I then approached, whispered some words of peace.
He looked upon me with mistrustful eye
And bursting into laughter, died.—See here
The finger of a God.—The wretch was given
By his high power to foul despair.—But what—
All warmth and colour from thy face are fled.—

**GUSTAVUS**
Oh leave me—hence—'Tis nothing: I am oft.
When weak in health, seized suddenly, as now.
But think'st thou not God would have pardoned him
If he in other things observed his law?

**XIMENES**
Pardoned—To Judas he never gave pardon—
This was his crime—treachery with murder joined—
But God is merciful.

**GUSTAVUS**
Oh mercy heavens!

**XIMENES**
Thy crimes I hope are not so great.
But now confess—that peace again may dwell
Within thy bosom—he whose tale I've told.
Dwells now with demons—plunged in wrathful flames
That scorching can't consume, he bums for ever.—

**GUSTAVUS**
Oh spare me, spare me! Urge me not—Lets forth
The cooling breeze will soon restore my health
And all I trust will then be well with me.

[Exeunt.


SCENE II.

Night. A Grove.

Enter **XIMENES**.

My heart feels full—it seems as if this done,
All else were ended—to exist were vain.
But yet I'm sick of working on this man
Who's strength is all in grief—who leaves no part
For mind or wit to act against.—But yet
I feel that I must on.—What is a smile
That the remembrance of its loss can work
Man thus.—Oh Eliza I have loved thee.
Thy love smother'd all other love, but then
It was so fair and beautiful a plant,
I could not wish my heart were more adorned.—
And then thy frowns, like heaven's wrath wither'd it
And changed the spot once so adorned to one
Whence naught but pestilence could issue forth,—
Thy image I have held within my heart
For years, and yet those years have not yet seen
Its colours fade. Thou'rt pictured to my mind
As when thou smilest first upon thy slave.
And these are moments to myself of bliss.—
But they are moments—for ne'er long remains
The image thus—again the frown's put on—
That frown, it too's imprinted here—that frown.

Oh! it! it was my blight. But then he suffers,
I am content—Ah no! my heart is like
The whirlpool of the sea.—Ship follows ship,
But all in vain—its stomach's large.—To see
Francesco thus, is something.—But from me
Must come a sting more deep than memory gives.

[Lowering of the sky, and distant thunder.

But I must hence—yon clouds with heavy step
Walk yon hill's side, and bring with them their wrath.
Making the night double—
Their edge, at intervals, is light as if
The glance of fabled Jove fell from his brow.
Guiding their steps. The ambient air seems dead,
And awed nature by this thrill silence seems
To wait chastisement—I will seek Francesco—
And, unobserved, will feast mine eyes on him.
As he shall crouch, dreading his God is come
To wreak his anger upon him, as if
A God would deign to gaze on aught below.

[Exit.

[A violent storm .— When ended.

[Enter **RINALDO**.

**RINALDO**
How sweet it is to breath this air—the storm
Which threatened but some moments since to hurl
All that now smiles around, to utter ruin.
Has cooled the breeze, and all the choiristers
Of night seem now with song to celebrate
Great nature's triumph o'er some fallen foe.
The smiling verdure round, now seems to wear
Attire most gay, for every leaf displays,
Radiant in silvery light of yon pale orb,
A thousand gems.
And the soft murmurs of the breeze invite
The soul with sounds harmonious to repose?—
But this blessed peace still seems to fly my breast,
Why shuns it me alone'—Ximenes means
Some foul deceit—else why not recognize
His former friend—save to procure his aid—
He thinks to make a tool—a tool—for what?
To act the lower parts of his revenge—
And why? to gain one who would scorn my vows.

If from her love I should attempt by wiles
And deep laid stratagems to rend her heart—
But who, at this dread hour, with heavy step.
With trembling limbs, and down cast look, comes here.

(He retires. Enter **GUSTAVUS**.

**GUSTAVUS**
What can it mean! can heaven then enter thus
Into those lesser cares for lowly man?
Yet thrice the dream as in sleep's soothing arms
Repose I sought, yet thrice the voice recurred—
God cannot think a father would obey!
What I! my hand! no, no! Anselmo's blood,
Tho' hell with galling racks should rend this frame—
Tho' all its flames conjoined should scorch these limbs.
Which at the best, are but fit food for flames.
Still my son's blood, though it were gentlest balm
Should not be shed to ease my aching wounds—
But can this mortal, feeble, frame resist
Its maker's will? An aged arm like this,
Can it resist the thunder of a God?—
Blood will have blood—the father of my friend
Calls for my son's blood—
I must obey! obey!—Nay, on this head,
Let, let, oh God! thy thunders fall—thy ire
Discharge its venom on me—I am old;
Long has this trunk looked for the cutting axe,
And if thou wilt, I will not from it shrink.
My son! and I to be his murderer!
Is this thy mercy God?—But why these doubts?
I still remembrance of it bear, and still
But tend to fix it on my mind more deeply.
As forth I issued the dark beetle winged
Its token sounding flight—the Vampire bat
Flitting around my head, impatient seemed
To wait my sacrifice—the brooding owl
Shrieked ominous, as forth I rushed to cool
My fevered brain. This more than hideous night
Was heaven's own choice, in which to speak its wrath
The plants around have scarcely raised their heads
After the tempest's rage—the lightning too
Has played foul havoc here—yon tree is scathed.
Like to my soul; perchance 'twas also done.
When he, who in his gayer youth did plant.
With careful hand, the seedling weakly shrub.
Was, by heaven's awful voice, like lightning struck.
But still it may not be—Why grieving thus?

It is but some dark phantom of foul hell.
Whose fiends more subtle prove than crouching snake.
I'll to Ximenes, he can hold converse
With heaven's pure inhabitants, for he
Has spent in virtuous deeds, and holy prayer
His many days. It may be God will deign
To speak through him—I will unto his cell
Betimes this morn—If peace may be my lot.
He may bestow't—if not, there still is death.

[Exit,

[RINALDO advances,

**RINALDO**
What was't he uttered—to destroy his son—
A voice he heard—'Tis surely this Ximenes;
For while I gazed intent upon the storm,
I saw him pass in haste, and soon again
With joyful step, return from whence the chambers
Of this Gustavus lay—And shall I see
A deed like this I when but a single word
Would save the world such crimes, shall I refrain
I will to Almoraddin, will to him
Impart whate'er I know—But this Ximenes
Once saved my life—I must to him disclose
I know his crimes; urge him by all that man
Is wont to hold most sacred on this earth.
To leave revenge, and let high heaven bestow
The punishment that's due to man on earth.

SCENE IV

Ximenes' Cell.

**XIMENES** alone.

**XIMENES**
Oh that th' event were known—this dull suspense.
This pleasing hope, thus mingling with the dread
Of failing in my wish, has caused the night
To seem to drag its lagging length along.
As if an whole eternity had lapsed
Between each turning of the flowing glass.
Thrice have I left my couch to view the stars,
And they in mockery of my wish, have seemed

To shine more brilliant as I issued forth—
And sleep has not its kind oblivion lent
One moment to my aching eyes, but fled
As if the troubled inmates of my breast
Were not congenial to its silent reign—
Oh! why to those who least require thine aid
Thus always fly? Why not the haunted mind
Visit at times—where peace so seldom dwells—
And heal with soothing balm, the deadly wounds
Of memory! The peasant needs thee not—
Sweet thoughts of years in virtuous actions spent,
Still make the night glide quickly by, and morn
Finds him uprisen, refreshed with peaceful thought
Of days well spent,—But I, whose life has been
Dark as the troubled seas o'ercast with clouds,
Whence the fierce thunders roll and lightnings flash.
Blasting at once the hopes of years—whose peace -
By treacherous friends has been destroyed—I want
Thy aid, which by thy sweet oblivious power.
Might cause a heaven in this sad breast, where dwells
A hell of thought—But wherefore ponder thus—
Let rather thoughts of how to be revenged
Upon deceitful man possess my mind—
Methinks this plot must meet with full success—
His superstition mingling with remorse
Has thrown him in my hands—and he is mine!
But ah! he comes! he comes! now shall I learn
How I succeeded? But I must not show
To outward view my joy—but as if wrapt
In meditation deep, appear absorpt.

[Enter **GUSTAVUS**.

**GUSTAVUS**
Hail holy father—I am come to seek
Some peace from thy most holy prayer—and ask
Thy counsel in a grief that weighs me down—
For all around speak loudly in the praise
Of thy great power to ease the troubled breast.

**XIMENES**
If God employs his slave in thy behalf,
Praise him, not me.

**GUSTAVUS**
Thus merit's always found.
Ever will modesty on virtue wait.—
But how shall I unfold, what I would say?

For when thou hearest a dream disturbs me thus,
Thou'lt call me fool—a simple, doating fool—
To credit thus frail phantoms of the mind,

**XIMENES**
A dream!
[Aside]
Oh then success has crown'd my hopes.—

**GUSTAVUS**
Thrice it recurred, and thrice methought a voice
Called upon me to sacrifice my son—
My only son.

**XIMENES**
Three times this dream recurred—
'Tis strange—'tis more than strange,—What I beheld
Is then too true—

**GUSTAVUS** [Holding him]
What did—didst thou then too—

XIMENES
Have I then let escape these foolish lips—
What did I say? Oh, I remember now—
If I am wrong—Almighty God! thou knowst—
Thou knowst the offence was done unwittingly.—

**GUSTAVUS**
But what sawst thou?

**XIMENES**
I must not, would not say—

**GUSTAVUS**
Then is it as I fear—more than I dread
It cannot be—wherefore conceal it thus?

**XIMENES**
I would not harrow up a father's heart,
Duties of peace are mine, not those of pain,—

**GUSTAVUS**
Oh quickly free me from this dread suspense—
More painful sure than aught that thou canst say.—

**XIMENES**
Why wilt thou to thy ruin madly rush?—

I could not bear to see a father's grief.

**GUSTAVUS**

I pray thee tell me—I entreat by him
Who on the rood died helpless for our sins.

**XIMENES**

Why rush thus madly on?—thou shalt repent
When 'tis too late; but since thou call'st on him
Whose badge I wear, I can no more refuse.

**GUSTAVUS**

Nay quickly speak—pray let me hear the whole.

**XIMENES**

Then listen to my tale, which I had wished
Might fast, in the recesses of my heart,
Have been for ever hidden.—
Last night, at that dread hour, when age reporteth
Damned ghosts, to seek repose awhile from hell.
Glide to the charnel house, to vest a form
Shaped of mephitick vapours from the dead,
And quickly passing seek their living friends.
And visit them with terror.—When first morn
And night begin to combat for their reign,
I yet was watching—wrapt in holy prayer—
Methought I heard a voice that bade me rise.—
I rose, when sudden to my wondering sight
The walls around seemed changed, and in their stead
I viewed as 'twere two living pictures placed.—
Amazed in mute astonishment I stood—
When lo! the self same voice called me to mark.
And what I saw relate to thee—for all.
That heaven's behest ordained, was yet undone.—

**GUSTAVUS**

And what sawst thou?

**XIMENES**

Here—on the left—here painted I beheld
A more than heaven—I saw thee happy there,
Thy face with sweetness bright, as if from joy
Content arose—and with thee walked thy son.
Through groves so rich, no words can e'er describe
Their beauty.—Flowers more sweet, than those that grow
In this vast orb, seemed to arise, where trod
Your airy feet.—Their odour spread around—
Ne'er did I think such pleasure to receive

Through any sense.—Angels, like cherub boys,
Flitted around and ministered your wants,
While nymphs, more delicate, than Moslems tell
Shall be their faithful Houries, softly danced
And beckoned to a gate, whence voices loud
Singing of nature's God, triumphant, came—
And soon from thence with glorious seraph choirs
Forth issued the meek Saviour of mankind—
And with him, one of form almost divine
Came running as a spouse into thy arms.
Wrapt in such splendour, eyes unpurified
Could not the brightness bear—I bowing fell.
When I again raised up my head 'twas vanished—
The other still remained.—But ask no more
'T would harrow up a very monsters' heart
To hear the rest.

**GUSTAVUS**
Nay let me hear the whole,

**XIMENES**
Where stands that wall, the other picture rose,
And there, as if life dwelt within, I saw
A murky sulphurous abode, light up
With blue and lurid flames, that never die.
The cries of those tormented and their scoffs
Still sound upon my ear and freeze my blood.
Gazing some time upon this scene, I saw
Thy son pursue thee through the scorching caves
Of this deep vast abyss.—With hellish joy.
With thongs of lead, he smote thy naked back.
Where loathing worms suckt up the dropping blood_
Anselmo cried, as each hard blow he dealt.
"Why let me wed that Moslam infidel?
Why not, as heav'n ordained, not take my life?"
While demons leaping round laughed thee to scorn.
And with loud echoing shouts applauded him—
But most I noted one in human shape
Whose stifled laugh made me to shrink—it seemed
I know not how, to be that form I'd seen
Upon the sepulchre.—But with trembling limbs
Struck with deep horror, back I shrunk aghast
And all was gone—

[**GUSTAVUS** stands transfixt with horror.

But look not thus cast down
Perchance 'tis but a phantom of the brain.

**GUSTAVUS**

May it? thou wouldst but soften what I feel.

**XIMENES**

Oh, would I could!
God's finger here is too, too manifest.
We could, nay dare not, thus shewn, resist.

**GUSTAVUS**

No! no! I will—I will not stain these hands.
My son shall live.—I—I will dare e'en God.

**XIMENES**

Ah, rash man! know'st thou not these impious
Are registered in heaven.—Thy son too's joined [words
The vision tells in thine own fate.

**GUSTAVUS**

'Tis true!

**XIMENES**

But go, retire, seek solitude awhile,
Then offer up to God thy humble prayer
That he may deign to grant thee his pure light;
And if thou feelest after this, the visions
Bear the dread stamp of truth, thou must obey.

**GUSTAVUS**

I will to prayer for strength to do his will;
Ximenes, pray for me; thy prayers to heaven
Like incense go, because thy heart is pure—
They sure are heard; but mine serve but the more
T' excite my angry God. But I'll not think.
My thoughts are maddening and my brain is weak.

[Exit.

**XIMENES**

All favours still my plans! fool that he is!
He knew not, wrapt in sleep, the voice was mine.
It almost seems the fickle goddess bowed
Obsequious to my will, and would at once
Make sweet amends for all the wildest freaks
That she has played on me. But most her smiles,
I fear, are false, when in impatient haste
They are on man bestowed.—I must not slack
My vigilance, but prove I'm not unworthy

Of her good will, by careful guard and watch
O'er her blind gifts. How sweet must be revenge!
When but the hope alone that it is ours
Can calm the ruffled mind, and ease the sting
Implanted in our breast by direst woes.
He shall in his son's blood imbue his hands;
But weak-eyed justice shall not sieze my foe;
He shall yet live, shall live to know his friend.
Holy Ximenes. Couldst thou now, revenge!
Put on some form that's sensible to touch,
In heart-felt joy I'd hug thee to my breast;
Now that I am wedded to thee, thou appearest
More lovely far than beauteous budding spring.
When first on nature shines the vernal sun;
But though thy fairer form should sudden change
To one like winter, though thy eyes were bleared.
Thy skin more wrinkled and more parched than hell
Has made Megera's—I would hug thee still.
Take thee as mine own bride; for as thy dower
Thou bring'st my foe's blest fall. If I could view
But mingling with the horror at his son
Dead at his feet, some part of that he'll feel.
When he shall know Orlando spurred him on,
I should indeed be blest. It cannot be;
His hand would instant end his, his hated life.
He still must suffer—still must feel remorse—
His breast—but I must watch him—I will go
And hang around his nest as if I were
A mother anxious for her brood, and let
None save those I will approach his door.

[Exit.


ACT V

SCENE I

Gustavus' Garden,

**XIMENES** and **RINALDO** meet.

**XIMENES**
Congratulate, rejoice with me, Rinaldo,
Again thou mayst acknowledge me, for now
I know myself again, the same who once
In fashion's gayest trappings proudly walked

With head erect that spoke the fearless heart.
And honour spotless as my gleaming sword.
Once more since youth's too well remembered days
My heart is light as then.

**RINALDO**
I came not here
To share thy joys; perfidious were the arts
That wronged my confidence, and made thy friend
The weak accomplice of the blackest crimes;
But think not that thy fiend-like soul could make
Me still thy tool; I am not fallen so low;
Rinaldo is unchanged; his ready hand
Put forth at friendship's call, must still refuse
Those services which friendship should not ask.

**XIMENES**
'Tis well!
[Aside]
He wavers, talks of virtue,
What opposite intentions brought us here!
Thou wouldst reproach, I would assist a friend;
I've had thy will, though not employed by me.
And tho' repented now; still in my mind
I will remember thy kind wishes, still
Will aid thy love.—The fair Euphemia's thine.

**RINALDO**
Why mock me unless thus, to make me feel
Some portion of thy pangs; well, well thou know'st
I cannot hope she ever will be mine,
But like the thirsty traveller I am doomed
To see the bourne of all my hopes and want
The power to reach the wished for living fount

**XIMENES**
But why at least not strive to gain thy hopes?

**RINALDO**
Thou know'st I would, for her, most gladly dare
Dangers of every various frightful form;
I'd dare the treacherous deep, the battle's roar,
Would stand unmoved though with their angry eyes,
Lions should glance and with wide open jaws
Should wait with seeming joy to sieze their prey.

**XIMENES**
And wilt thou not be silent for the prize?

**RINALDO**

Couldst thou Euphemia to my arms but promise,
I would not ope my lips to blab of this,
Though she herself should smiling ask it me,

**XIMENES**

This eve, ere yon bright sun shall hide his head
Within the gilded sea—she shall be thine—
Anselmo's then to meet his love.—No more—
If but my plan succeeds, we'll meet again—
I have a bark hard by, which waits my orders
To hoist its sails and seek that happy clime,
Where we the blissful days of youth enjoyed.—
Get but some slaves to aid in seizing her—
And she is thine.—Some few there may be found,
Who liberty to gain, will more than friends—
Will this content thy friendly honesty?

**RINALDO**

Content, ask the wild Moor, if when aroused
From sleep, he sees the royal tyger crouch
Intent with sudden spring on him to leap—
Ask him, if some bold ven'trous hand should lay
The keen eyed foe dead at his trembling feet.
If he's content?—

**XIMENES**

Then seek some willing slaves,
And e'er the shades of eve, with dubious light
Shall mellow nature's varied tints, be here—
And, if the fickle goddess fails us not.
We both succeed. But pray be well aware
That honesty may blast the fairest hopes.

**RINALDO**

At last before my wildered, aching sight,
The wished for haven rises into view—
If but a prosperous breeze inflate our sails,
I soon again shall see my native shores,
And visit once again those ancient seats.
Where infancy was passed.—I shall lead her
Whom with desparing thought I long have loved
O'er those fair spots so rich with memory.—
But I must hence, and seek some captive's help
To seize Euphemia—Seize my love! Oh fool!
To think she can e'er love thee, if by force
She's dragged from all she holds most dear—And thus?

Do I then keep those vows made fore the shrine
To virtue?—I will break these shameful bonds—
Will save Gustavus from his guilt, and spare
Euphemia—But I feel my love would bid
Me not obey.—But if I save for her.
What here she holds most dear—she'll pity me
And chance may heave a sigh o'er my sad fate—
I'll to Almoraddin and will disclose
Whate'er I know—I cannot then retract.

[Exit.


SCENE II

Gustavus' Anti-chamber.

Enter **GUSTAVUS**.

**GUSTAVUS**
Ah whither can I fly—I feel as if
Impelled to plunge into eternity.—
But can eternity afford relief
To guilt like mine? If even here my crimes
Have mantled nature in a robe of gloom—
Dimm'd the effulgence of the noon-day sun,
And made me find, in ev'ry warbling note
Of heaven's gay choiristers notes of reproach,
In every rustling leaf a sound, which seems a voice
That bids me fly—for here a tainted thing
May never dwell—can then eternity
Receive and shelter one so deeply cursed 'I
But why, as if or heaven or hell could give
A refuge from God's wrath, such madness utter?
This mother earth seems trembling with my weight
And frowns as if to urge this desperate hand
To ease it of this vile and loathsome load—
But why endeavour to divert my thought
From resting on my child? It must be done—
What must be done? All have with God conspired
To force me to his will.—
But yet my son may yield! oh yes. I'll kneel—
My prayers shall move him to forego his love
And ransom me from this—

[Enter **ANSELMO** who embraces him.

Fly instant hence—
Touch not this form scathed by the fire of God,
Lest lightnings glance from ev'ry limb to blast thee.
My son Oh yes! it is my son—

**ANSELMO**
Father!

**GUSTAVUS**
I know what thou wouldst say—I'm cursed of God!
I know it; tell me something else—My son!
My son! if not that thou wouldst share in this
My punishment; if not that all thou viewest
Should act as 'twere a mirror to thy soul
And show thy figure in form so hideous,
That thou wouldst shut thine eyes and fly in horror
Of thine own image—if from all around
Thou wouldst not hear the maledictions deep,
That curse thy presence as the bane of nature,
Abjure the passion that offends thy God.

**ANSELMO**
Oh father! rave not thus, thy restless eyes
Speak madness wilder than thy hurried voice.

**GUSTAVUS**
This is not madness tho' my words may wear
Its semblance. Oh my son! Oh! sacrifice—
Thy father begs thee—sacrifice thy love—

**ANSELMO**
Forsake Euphemia? rather let me die.

**GUSTAVUS**
Die! who informed thee?—Die! who seeks thy life?

**ANSELMO**
I said not that such danger threatened me—

**GUSTAVUS**
What have I said? 'twas nought—'twas but my raving—
But if thou wouldst not cut the few short hours
That still remain allotted to my life—
Obey the will of heaven and thou'lt avert
The heaviest curse from off thy sire's last days.

**ANSELMO**
These are but phantoms of a troubled mind.

Thy body lab'ring with disease, affects
Thy reason too—send for some skilful leach—

**GUSTAVUS**
'Tis too true, my son! These aged limbs are weak
And scarcely can support this shattered frame.
But think not that disease has slowly sapped
My vital powers—My wasting strength decays
Obedient to the doom pronounced on high
Against my guilt. Think not, pray my son.
That what I say is but the troubled fancy
Of a weak mind diseased—But grant my prayer.

**ANSELMO**
Father my word is given—my honour pledged;
Wouldst thou by such a breach of solemn faith
Devote my name to endless infamy—

**GUSTAVUS**
Oh mercy God! Return from this mad folly.
A father kneels before his son—my son!
Thou then art moved; come to my aged arms—
Behold these tears—change them to tears of joy.

**ANSELMO**
My father! I'm thy son—thou wouldst not have
Thy son be pointed at, as one disgraced—

**GUSTAVUS**
Then wilt thou not for me cast off her love?

**ANSELMO**
My father! strive not thus to rend her love
From my weak heart; I love thee much, my sire.
And would not wish that thy old age should pass
In aught but happiness—but thou thyself.
When, happy in each other's love, we twine
Around thy neck, wilt own that heaven could not
Intend such love should ere be broke by man—
Seeing thy son thus happy in his love
Cannot the thread of my dear father's life
Ere cut. God's will can ne'er decree injustice—

**GUSTAVUS**
Canst thou perceive the cause of aught that acts
Below?—and how canst thou pretend to say
Where God is just?—God is but too just,—
My son, wilt thou not willing expiate

A part of what has been decreed against me?

**ANSELMO**
Most willingly, but heaven cannot approve
A crime should expiate a crime, and yet
Thou askest of me to break a plighted oath.

**GUSTAVUS**
And canst thou then refuse thy sire this boon?

**ANSELMO**
I must not grant what is a sin to grant.

**GUSTAVUS**
My son! but you shall have that name no longer.
May all the—No! no! I cannot curse my son—
The Almighty's curse is e'en too much already—
Nay! hold me not—Thou know'st not what is done.
And more what misery will follow hence.

[Exeunt.

SCENE III

A grove in Gustavus's gardens.

Enter **GUSTAVUS**.

**GUSTAVUS**
And must I strike?—Must then my only son
Yield up his life, beneath a father's blow?
Had heaven then no means to castigate
His slave for crimes, but this? I dare not now
To look around—the murmurs of the stream.
The softest whisper of the playful breeze.
Cause me to start with horror at myself—
I shun the eyes of all; for if perchance
They glance upon me and mine eyes meet theirs,
Trembling I seem to shrink within myself,
And wish some rock would from its basement torn
With their poor self my 'palling terrors end—
It seems as if some guilt I dare not view
Thus spurred me on.

[Gazing on the dagger in his hand.

Oh! hide thy hated form;
Render thyself invisible to man.
And let my eyes not see thy blasting point.
Can I then hold with hand so little firm
This cursed dagger?—Yet it feels as bound
By some officious demon to my hand.

[Seeing them at a distance.

The wheels of fate move rapidly; they come—
Oh, those sweet smiles will soon, too soon, be changed;
Changed! and by whom? By him who gave thee birth.
Whose happiest hours were those, when on his knee
He held thee fondling; and whose every hope,
Whose every wish was centered in thy good.
But now, how changed! The hand that loved to guide
Thy infant steps, and trace thy mother's face
Upon thy lineaments—must now, alas!
Must now deliver thee to death's embrace—
For so the Almighty power above decrees.—
I will not!—hence!—Will not!—I must! I must!
Such mercy would be false—would doom my son
For an eternity to God's dread anger—
And has not God decreed?—What can I do?
Oh, God! if such thy will, why not erase
Each trace of past affection?—why not shed
Oblivious dews o'er memory's dearest page.
And blot his long-loved name from every line?
Oh, that my arm ere yet it strikes may fall
Withered and impotent! But see—to whet
My failing anger—how the syren meets
His close embrace, and o'er him hangs deceitfid,
As erst o'er Eve the wily serpent hung
So witching, that she smiled at her own ruin,—
My God! my God! thou sendest them entwined
Before my sight, to urge my flagging purpose.—
They come!—I am resolved.—Be firm, my heart!
But I'll retire and watch my time to strike.—

[Retires.

[Enter **ANSELMO** and **EUPHEMIA**.

**EUPHEMIA**
Only four days! thou mock'st me surely love!
So brief a space could ne'er contain the world
Of anxious cares, that have oppressed my peace.
And made thy absence seem eternity.

But having thee, they all are gone.

**ANSELMO**
Nor have I panted less than thou, sweet love.
To meet again—but as such happy hours
Must now be few and stolen—let me at once
Disclose the fearful thoughts that rend my heart.

**EUPHEMIA**
What means my love? Has slander's venom'd tongue
Assailed Euphemia's fame? Have I done aught
To raise suspicion or incur reproach?

**ANSELMO**
Canst thou offend the heart that thus adores thee?

**EUPHEMIA**
But well thou know'st they say that love is blind.
And needs another hand to guide his steps;
And hence is oft through other's faults misled.

**ANSELMO**
But can the love I bear to thee be blind.
When dazzling light beaming from those dark eyes
Illumines all around? But wilt thou not
Cast far away my love?

**EUPHEMIA**
I cast thy love away!—Could ivy leave
The friendly oak to which it clings for life,
Still I could not survive thy love.

**ANSELMO**
If he
E'en from whose stock I sprung be self confessed
A most vile villain—should such loveliness
Owe its support to me i Stung by remorse
My father owned his crimes—but spare my sire.—
Canst thou still love me after this?

**EUPHEMIA**
I'd love thee
Though father, friends, and all, proved to myself
The greatest foes, and with unhallowed lips
Should foulest poison breathe o'er my fair fame;
Thou art no wretch thyself, and still my love
Would cling more close to thee,

**ANSELMO**
But couldst thou wed a wretch like me?

**EUPHEMIA**
If it be thus indeed as thou hast said,
That thy fair fame is gone, thou wilt need
The more some comforter; I'll comfort thee.

**ANSELMO**
Then art thou mine indeed; nor father's tears,
Nor storms that man can cause, shall part us more.

**EUPHEMIA**
In humblest captive's cot we'll live content.
If they should thwart our happiness.

**ANSELMO** [They embrace]
My: love!

**GUSTAVUS** [Advancing aside]
I now must strike—my heart begins to yearn—
My hand grows nerveless.—Oh, my son! my son!

[Strikes hut only wounds him slightly;—stabs himself, and is caught in his son's arms.

**ANSELMO**
What, my—my father thou!

**GUSTAVUS**
Reproach me not;
My heart is nearly rent, to punish crimes
More black than night.—God forced me on to this,

**ANSELMO**
Oh God! but why reproach my father now?
Thy blood flows unrestrained, and none are near.
And thou, my love!

[Seeing **EUPHEMIA** fainted.

Oh, help! help! there! help! help!

**GUSTAVUS**
Regard me not. I could not credit thee,
Ximenes! thou wert wrong,—God could not wish—

**ANSELMO**
Ximenes! what then, was it he who caused

Thine arm to rise against Euphemia's life.

**GUSTAVUS**
'Twas not at her I aimed, 'twas at thyself.

**ANSELMO**
Thy son! But thou art faint—help! help!

[Enter **ALMORADDIN**, **XIMENES**, **RINALDO**, and others.

**ALMORADDIN**
Am I
Then come too late?—my daughter too is slain!

XIMENES
What, have I failed of my intent? He lives.

**ANSELMO**
Sieze quickly that vile wretch! If thou wilt speak,
Say what could move thee to this dreadful crime,
Which I would not my lips should even utter.
Lest that the winds should waft it up to heaven
And bring from thence destruction on our heads.

**XIMENES**
He shall declare the cause.—View, heartless fool.

[Throwing off his cowl.

Canst thou remember me? I'm Count Orlando.

**GUSTAVUS**
Hide me!—Oh, let me not behold that form
I feel I cannot live—Orlando—I—
Have wronged thee—nay, I did thee more than wrong.
But did I merit this? Oh, ves! I did.—
Those sunken eyes—that deeply grief-worn face—
They tell me much;—I cannot hope for pardon.

**XIMENES**
Pardon! my foes I ne'er forgave, and thou
Shalt thou then hope it? no! this dress— this garb
Were but assumed, my vengeance on thy head
With interest to wreak, for my lov'd sire,
For my lost love—

**GUSTAVUS**
Art thou not satisfied? Is not revenge

Yet sated in that breast?

**XIMENES**
No! Yet sated? no!
If all that I had hoped had followed hence—
If I had seen thee infamous on earth.
Thy conscience like a worm, gnawing thy heart,
Thy dying son pouring another curse
Most bitter to thy soul on thy grey hairs;
I should not have been satisfied.—Thou stole
To thy embrace through filthy wantonness
Eliza—her I loved.—Satisfied!

**ANSELMO**
Stop!
Give not such damned licence to thy tongue.
My father's spirit's flown!—Lead him from hence—

**RINALDO**
Lead him from hence—deprive his hands of means
Wherewith to set his loathed spirit free
From that accursed body.

**XIMENES**
What Rinaldo
Leads me to death! I once led death from him.

[Exit guarded.

**EUPHEMIA** [Recovermg]
Ah! where am I! Oh! my loved Anselmo!
But saw I not the flashing steel descend—

**ANSELMO**
He lives! he lives, my child!

**EUPHEMIA**
Does he! Oh yes,
I see where I am now—'Tis heaven, and thou
Art some kind angel sent to sooth my grief;
Go, ask Mahomed—ask that he admit
Me where Anselmo is—I prithee ask.

ANSELMO
Do not speak thus, my dear Euphemia, see
Anselmo's here—

**EUPHEMIA**

Art thou indeed then faithful?
Has heaven then granted what my soul desired?
Am I to live with thee? Oh! shall I wait
Both morn and night upon thee?—Shall I weave
Of these fair roses, garlands for thy head?
And soon, as from this wide expanse, the stars
By the bright rising sun are driven,
May I a wreath of never fading flowers
Place on thy locks?

**ANSELMO**
Oh! add not to my woes—
Seest thou not this fair grove, where oft we sat
Together, viewing nature's fairest works?

**EUPHEMIA**
Why still deceive me? Have I lost thy love?
If so—I'll leave thee here to seek with these
Some fairer love—but then thou canst not find
One, who will love thee with a love like mine.

**ANSELMO**
My best, my kindest love—Oh! leave me not.

**EUPHEMIA**
And does it please thee that I should remain?
Oh! happiness indeed—Embrace thy love.

**ALMORADDIN**
Let us conduct her hence—some rest may sooth
Her troubled mind.

**ANSELMO**
Let us from hence my love—

**EUPHEMIA**
Let us to yonder bower and leave these here,
We want no such companions—farewell—come.

[Exeunt.

SCENE THE LAST

A Dungeon.

**XIMENES.**

**XIMENES**
Is then my course cut short, and must I now
Still in the noon of life,—ah! must I leave
All hopes of fame behind, and quit those scenes.
Where oft my soul would dream of future bliss?
But why shun death? What ties have I to earth?
Where all shall look with eyes of scorn upon me—
How could I now come forth in sight of man.
While yet this stain's unwashed—this foulest stain
Oh why revenge didst thou forsake me here?
In hopes of thee, some few, few moments passed,
I was most blessed: an outcast now from men
I'm doomed to be to them a gazed-at show;
But shall they then expose Orlando, me!
To wrinkled hags and old grey sinning heads?
No! here is, what can speedily do more.
Than I dare name. Oh death! of what art thou
The harbinger?—Whither do these wide gates
Open to entrance lead—Eternity!
But why dread that? Already with dark wings
It hovered o'er my birth, my youth, my life—
Eternity waits not for death, to spread
Its influence o'er our soul—It ne'er begun
As it ne'er ends—But why dream thus? 'tis folly—
This little draught will ease my aching heart
Of all its rankling cares. But with these weeds
The soil is carried too—It will end all—
All I what annihilate this very self?
Oh then shall nought remain, but this vile corse
And that too food for worms? Oh, that swift time
Might back revolve and bring again those dreams,
Which once would cheer me under fancied ills;
Oh, dreams of immortality! why hence!
But can I wish they should to me return?
Eternity! eternity of pain!
Some little time from hence and then, Orlando
Will be no more—His name too gone, or worse;
Known but as a foul meteor of the night.
On which, from dark sulphureous caves below.
Pale Hecate with her blasting spells might ride.
Peace! peace! thou silly babbler conscience! Peace!

[He drinks the poison.

Already do I feel it working here;
Creation soon shall all be lost to me—

Soon shall I wrapt in sleep have all forgot,
In sleep so sound, that none disturb my rest;
For what is death but sleep, whence none can wake?—
My mind at last shall calm repose enjoy—
Ah!
[Starts]
— but thou wilt not suffer peace to reach me,
Thou beckonest me away—I come, I come—
Yes sure it was, 'twas I who caused that wound—
Why need to bare thy breast? What oh! why then
Revenge! I yet am satisfied, content.
Do those flames burn thy unrelenting heart?
But spare me! oh! point not thy finger thus
Flames issue thence which scorch my very soul.

[Enter **ALMORADDIN**, **ANSELMO**, and **DOMINIC**.

Oh! oh! are then more come to help thee—Ah!
What thou too there? But why that smile at me!
Yet, yet these flames torment thee too—Ha! Ha!

[He falls laughing.

**ANSELMO**
Then has the wretch escaped the vengeance due?

**XIMENES**
Why, yet listen—hear me—was it not well?
What thou too frownst, thou crime inspiring fiend?
Speak, speak, didst thou not spur me on to this?
Why seize me thus? Ah spare! I come, I come;
But yet Eliza fly not thus from me—
Thou shrink'st from my burnt breast—I burn, I love thee,—
Thou wilt not hear—Yet flames torment him too.

[Dies.

**ANSELMO**
Has he then mock'd our power? and justice still
Bears sway above?

**DOMINIC**
Tho' he has fled from shame.
And shunned the punishment of man below
Still shall he feel a deeper blush of shame.
When knowing all the greatness of his crimes.
He'll hear them loudly blazed, when bursts the tomb,
And the last call shall wake us to our doom.

[Exeunt.


## THE WREATH

To —


O thou! for whom this humble Wreath is formed,
Not from the flow'rs that deck the lowly meads,
But from those flow'rs Apollo's ray has warmed.
On which the dance Thalia often leads.

Despise it not, because the flow'rs are dull.
Or ill arranged—my heart beat high with fears;
My eyes with love's despairing tears were full.
Looking to pluck the robe Parnassus wears.

For since thy image burst upon my sight,
My fancy paints but heaven as a meet place,
Where thou couldst dwell, and I a mortal wight.
But pine to see the spot, which thou may'st grace.
Despise then not my Wreath, thy beauty blame alone#
And let thy lover's sufferings for the crime atone.


## WRITTEN AT THE GRIMSEL

### IN SWITZERLAND

In vain I seek these solitary rocks,
Which seem to leave no track upon their side
For man to tread upon.—These during blocks
Of the world's masonry, o'er which storms glide
Powerless, unmoved stern in their might yet stand,
And leave no room for man's destructive hand,—
Yet I am vainly hid within their breast,
They cannot breathe on me their quiet rest—
Man's passions will intrude, man's wants assail
E'en me—whose tongue is dead, save when the gale
Strikes on my ear with harsh but plaintive note,
Exciting words which mingling with it float.
And make the echoing rocks respond my grief,
As if I'd take from sympathy relief.—

But vain illusion! e'en fond hope is dead.
And all save angry passions hence have fled,
Angry with fates, who gave but visions' food
Unto my mind, when, foolish youth! I woo'd
Their smiles.—Oh why, tormenting fiend-like sprites
Thus let me go midst passion's, folly's flights,
Midst men in fine, with visions in my mind.
That I midst them might friendship, virtue find?—
Oh why still in my soul, those hopes of fame,
Which brought the sigh when busy morning came
Stealing from midnight lamp those studious hours
Midst which I cull'd the various fragrant flowers
That grow where'er the Muses' feet may tread.
And which I hoped enwreath'd might deck my head
And bright with glorious gleam, might shining there.
For ages show an undiminish'd lair—
Why make me strike the lyre as if I felt
That happiness in some vale lonely dwelt,
Waiting for me, when from my sounding lyre
Such strains should flow as fit a poet's fire—
Why let me read th' historic page, where's told
In lying tales, that men could freedom hold.
That men in ancient times of Grecian sage
Gainst meaner passions constant war would wage.

But these, e'en these, I might forgive, forget.
But why that vision send?—Was it to whet
The point of all your stings? That vision sent
Of one so meekly bright, if the moon lent
Her soothing ray, she had not been more fair,
Nor could she be more light, if from the air
Yon blushing lovely cloud, that seems to lave
In the sun's western ray, ere in the wave
He sinks to rest; not if yon cloud came down
To vest around its lightness as a gown
Upon her limbs, could she appear more light—
And, as she pass'd, wending her airy flight
To whence she came, methought I heard a sigh
As wafted on the breeze come from the sky,
Methought I saw grief passing o'er her brow
As she gazed on me, chance she wished to show
She felt my pains—But I awoke, and lo!
The morn, stealing upon the upland brow.
Had rayed herself in mist as if to hide
In pity her light rosy glorious pride
Seeming as tho' she wished me still to dream.
And not to break this only joyous gleam.

Fool that I was! I let that image rest
Upon my mind—I hugg'd it to my breast—
Forgetting that such forms to heaven alone
Are given to hover round the Godhead's throne—
For oh! I vainly yet must seek this haunt,
Which solitude to make its dwelling's wont.
I cannot fly that beauteous form—one time
I saw her on yon beetling rock—I climb—
Bounding from crag to crag, I haste to clasp
Her airy shape—the mist has mock'd my grasp—
And high on tow'ry pinnacle I stand
Gazing on scenes subdued by man's foul hand.
To fly the sight of which I'd sought this cave
In hopes of rest their absence never gave—
Oft, oft, I'm wak'd from slumbers by her voice.
Which seems with her to call me to rejoice;
But all that strikes my ear is the harsh sound
Of the lone breeze that wanton beats around.

Oh! why then fliest thou Time! with slacken'd wing?
Why not with thee old blear-eyed age e'en bring?
Its whit'ning snows would drop upon my head.
At last 'twould lead me to a quiet bed.—
Or if e'en years should pass, length'ning my age,
Ere death my foes in battle might engage,
Still hoping to begin my journey's toil,
I might with pleasure gaze, leaving this coil,
On all that once had reft me of my peace.
Conscious I went, where they'd no longer teaze.


SONNET.

On Seeing —, 1818

Last night I saw that vision once again
Which in my early youth view'd through a dream
Threw o'er my life the only bright'ning gleam
That heaven, it seem'd, upon my life would deign.

Yes, yes, what fancy pictur'd to my mind
Exists and decks this earth—around her spread
Is light so soothing, where her feet may tread
It seems that even grief repose might find.
Her pains thus sooth'd in sleep—but sleep is weak
In soothing power, when near her playful smile—
And when her eyes such soothing words can speak.

E'en grief forgets that sleep might chance beguile
Her woes—and that on him she call'd for rest
'Gainst pains that restless strive within her breast,


## MY DREAM

'Tis said that dreams eome true, if it be so
I well may die, while yet —'s breath
Leaves on my feverish cheek its warmer glow—
For sleep calls spectred grief to sight—yet death,
That long, long hop'd for harbinger of peace,—
As on the sleepy wave the wanton breeze.
Which playing midst the cords ard flapping sails.
Yet in sufficient strength to waft him fails.
Oft mocks the anxious sailor when in sight
'Of all he views or thinks of with delight—
But seems to play around and sport his dart
Through air, though I expose my grieving heart
Unto his aim.—If, fates! 'tis your decree.
Then I must bow—for where from you to flee!
But why foretaste of evil ere its time
Inflict upon your slave I—What heinous crime
Has merited such pain? Why when fair sleep
On me, so joy'd with hopes, began to creep
Why send that dream?

In which I stood midst rocks.
Midst barren vale, midst heaven-aspiring blocks
Of time-enduring granite—mountains rear'd
Their cloud-embosom'd heads and then appear'd
Above striking the firmament; their sides
Were loaded with the weight of frozen tides.
Huge blue glaciers.—As once the milk I've seen
From mother's breast froze ere it fell between
The lips of hungry babe, so seem'd these waves
To mock the valley's want.—No river laves
Its sides so barren bleak and desolate—
Yet still it seem'd their melting to await.
For there were tracks of waters' furious rage
Which seem'd the fruitful mould, in past-by age.
From off this world's huge limbs, thence to have lav'd-
It seem'd as if those pinnacles had rais'd
Their head to heaven, least like the valley raz'd
By water's rage, they prove its barren grief.—
But vain, for they too sear'd, found no relief
From clouds or heaven—yet had they look'd up white

With frost and aged snows ere man saw light.

It seem'd as if for years I'd trod this ground
Sear'd like the rocks—lone as the valley round—
With weary mind baffled in search of cause
Worthy of action, worthy of applause,
With weary body—feet and hands cut deep
From running o'er the rocks, climbing the steep;
For oft my wanton wayward fancy show'd
Upon some high-rear'd cliff where sunbeam glow'd,
A vision.—Then I would bound and climb—but gain'd
'Twas but another pang, and I retain'd
But bleeding wounds.—Yet these heedless were borne,
I car'd not though my body mangled, torn.
Were scarr'd—

But once it seem'd—one lovely morn
When e'en the rocks, the vale, the mount, had borne
The gilding ray of the bright sun—a voice.
Which Echo sounded too, bade to rejoice
My lonely heart—for happiness was near—
Nature began a lovely green to wear.
And lo! from the glad east a heavenly form
Came radiant with soft silvery light—no storm.
Pent in the clouds, e'en by the moon was grac'd
With ray so fair around its edge, while paced
Its fury o'er the wave as she whose eye
Rais'd, as it glanc'd, a scene, wherein to vie
Nature's proud gifts began—here forest grows
Showing beneath its sheltering wood, the rose
Cluster'd around the woodbine's climbing arms,
Here jessamines and lilies lend their charms
To lowly cot.—And as each step she'd take
Nearer to me, the playful breeze would shake
Th' approaching corn, the rising forest's pride—
Beneath this spreading mantle's various hue,
E'en rocks and snows were beauteous to the view—
But these were nothing.— She approach'd my side—
How shall I paint her charms? No poet's dream
E'er show'd a form so fair; no heav'nly gleam
Of prophet's fire could paint e'en Virtue's grace
With hues so chaste, though bright, as deck'd her face.
Oh! was it but the breeze that those words spoke,
"I! I am thine!"—For scarce she fell into my arms
When, as if from some fiend, I felt a stroke,
I saw another bear away her charms—
Yet I moved not—but slowly fainting fell—
And all around was lost.—

Why must I tell
Of what ensu'd—Oh! why was life thus spared?
I had died happy when those words I heard,
"I! I am thine."— But from the Glacier's breast
There rose a breath, that rous'd me from my rest,
And made me feel the blight of life.— It seem'd
As if since that fair form had on me gleamed,
I could not live.— Yet liv'd I on an age
The rocks were all enjoined no more to wage
War 'gainst my feet—no stone slipt from my foot—
Though I did tempt the precipice, which goat
Or chamois ne'er approach'd. 'Twas vainly tried.
In vain I ev'ry mountain goat defied.
My hands seem'd like the ivy's bending strings.
To clasp the rock; my feet seem'd to gain wings.—
I laid myself upon the avalanche;
But it would wait, till I was passed, to launch
Itself with noise of thousand thunders down
Into the vale, where I still strove to drown
My grief with tears.—

But I awoke and found
My pillow wet, my curtains strewn around—
'Tis true—'twas but a dream—yet doth it weigh
Upon my heart. I cannot drive away
Its heavy load. For if —'s lost—
Oh, no!—I must not think! Midst tempests tost
Hope smiling rose beyond the storm's dread frown.
Not e'en the stormy wave her form could drown.
And shall I here? Though all, e'en all may fail.
Still will I hope. For though hope's bliss be frail,
Yet greater joys no other fair could give.
Though she should deign my very slave to live.
And when that blow shall come, that fatal hour
May pass o'er ruined hopes fair fallen flow'r;
It shall not pass and see my falling tear,
But see its victim in my shrouded bier.


SONNET

To the Night


O Starry night! thou art most beauteous fair,
And I could gaze on thee, till my sight ached—
Thy cooling zephyrs play amidst my hair,

And cool my fever'd brain, which long has waked—
Such stillness seizes on the ear—the beams
Of yonder galaxy steal on the eye
With such soft soothing power—the whole it seems
Would bid us seek for heaven above that sky—
And hope for peace beyond that bright'ning zone.
Which seems to keep her near yon heav'nly throne;—
But still thou pleasest more, 'cause thou canst show
The image of —'s pow'r whence flow
Such magic words, as still man's stormy breast.
Such rays as sooth e'en mem'ry, future fears to rest.


## SONNET

### On being told that I was changed

I'm chang'd, aye chang'd indeed! The festal board
Was wont to cheer—but nothing now can gain
A passing smile, or transient bliss afford—
For I —'s love cannot obtain—
My comrades jeer and say a drop of dew.
From off the verge of midnight Hecate's broom.
Fell in my mouth, as grief those accents drew.
In which absorpt I wail'd my saddened doom—
Some tell me that of late a poisonous tear
From bleared old maid fell in the merry cup,
In which I pledged her love—which drop could bear
My senses down and bring grim madness up—
But I'm not mad, tho' dazzled now by her lov'd face,
As by the sun's bright disk, on all, her form I trace.


## SONNET

### On seeing a Dove nestled on —'s bosom

—with her gay and merry voice
Was causing- all around her to rejoice—
Her modest smile was cheering e'en my heart.
As sunbeam glads the prisoner in his cell,
Who feels no more of galling chains the smart.
While he can bask and look on where it fell—
Gazing on her I thought how he were blest
On whom such gladd'ning smile through life should shine.
When if on me they but a moment rest.

My sear'd heart beats and e'en forgets to pine—
To tell me more, a ring-dove saw her too,
And emblem of pure innocence it flew.
And in her bosom nestled close, remained,
Thinking it there congenial seat had gained.


## SONNET

To—

The other Eve, while sitting by the side
Of her for whom I sigh, but sigh unheard.
She bade me read the page in which 'twas tried
To tell in verse the pangs fond lovers shared.—
She knew not that those sorrow'd words express'd
The reader's pains—she gazed upon my face
When my voice shook, but feeling I repress'd.
She nothing in my eyes by hers could trace—
She bade me draw some figure in her book.
But I could not,—I tried a hero's brow—
My pencil fail'd—my treacherous hand but shook.
While love beneath the helm his face would show.
And if—knew I dar'd to love.
Spotless, she'd fear, some weakness hurl'd her from above.


## SONNET

To —

The sun fades daily on the dazzled eye;
And yon fair star, the harbinger of rest.
Ere the broad disk has sunk into the west,
Treads on its path and bids dull labour fly.—
The moon, though soothing be her silvery light,
Still wends her way across yon starry dome
With ever pauseless though majestic flight;
For sleep, deadner of woe, to man must come—
Yet thy fair image, ever Tore my sight.
Would ever seem incapable of change,—
For it so cheers my heart with soft delight,
It dares not from the lovely image range.
Lest pain and mental anguish seize again
Upon that throne where hope with thee is wont to reign.

## SONNET

### Oh seeing—lay my verses in her bosom

What! canst thou prize the foolish verse I give?
Caust thou,—, let my verses lay
Upon thy lovely breast? then I will live
And strive once more to sing some roundelay—

For if thou smilest on my humble rhyme
I will not sit content in idleness,
But will attempt a song worthy the clime.
Graced by the bard who sang of Troy's distress.—

Late I despised my lyre, I knew not then
That its light note could please —'s ear.
And I car'd not for vain applause of men—
But thou, whose glance my heart alone can cheer.
Hast praised its lay.—That praise has caus'd, I seize
My lyre again, in hope my love to please.


## SONNET

### To my native land

Adieu! my native land, adieu! Thy smiles no more
Shall sooth thy child—thy very charms increase
His pain—Adieu! I leave thy richer shore,
And fly where'er the wanton winds may please—
I late enraptur'd gazed upon thy leas.
And fancy lent her never-failing store
To deck the cot embosomed by those trees
I lov'd—and nature fancy's tinsel wore—
But now I look around and all thy charms
Call bitter memory up—yet I but see
The self same cottage's smoke—the sun but warms
The landscape erst I viewed, and decks the tree
Beneath whose shade I lay the other eve,
When hope still linger'd in the heart it now doth leave.


### To —

'Tis vain to struggle—let my grief have way.
Let the winds waft my sorrow as they play
Around —'s path—or rather bear
My griefs to nature's bosom—rocks will share
Their pain and echo back the plaintive note—
The sound that tells my grief, may even float
On the wave softened as it falls from lyre.
That speaks its master's soul—but she, whose fire
I bear, consuming' life—she will not hear
Its tale—she laughs at all the pain I bear—
But yet 'tis vain—her frown cannot efface
The image that e'en tardy death shall trace
Upon my heart, when he shall come to fill
The law, and ease my heart in spite of fate's dread will.

I tried to laugh and smile on all around.
But then my smile was like the Iris wound
About the storm's dread boundary—my heart
Still raged within, though round my lips the part
Of acting joy was on—thus men adorn
The marble tombs, whither from hope they're borne
To vile corruption's dire abode—the smiles
Of golden cherubs deck the gorgeous piles.
And cheat mankind, but not the scoffing worm
Which laughs while feeding on ambition's form.

But I can write no more—my peopled brain
Pours out such spectres in successive train.
My mind grows wildered, and my lyre can't speak
The various lash with which they vengeance wreak
Upon the heart—that vent'rous dar'd to love
Her, heaven sent to show what beings liv'd above.


SONNET

To my Lyre.

I dare no more to strike thee, lovely lyre!
My brain grows wilder'd, and my heart but grieves
Thou canst not speak the love-consuming fire.
That burns my heart, mine eyes of tears bereaves.
E'en, e'en that smile, which, like the evening dew
That falls upon the parched field, would smooth
My furrow'd brow, as round her lips it flew.
Now fails in power my writhing pains to sooth;
For grim despair has seiz'd upon my breast.

And laughs at its own ruin, scoffing me—
It snatches in its boney clutch from rest
My sinking heart, and mocking points at thee—
Then go, let the winds whisper midst thy strings.
Thy note no longer soothing pleasure brings.


## SONNET

To my Friend.

Weep not, my friend! dry up thy flowing tear;
Though broken-hearted on my couch I lay,
Think not that hastening death brings with it fear.
It opens fore my sight a joyous way.—
I leave upon this couch my cares, my grief;
They follow not beyond these passing scenes;
And though my life has flown without relief.
Death from the breast of care man quickly weans.
Nay, more, I may, perchance, soaring above,
View her, when she shall hear her lover's fate.
Come weeping o'er the bier of one, whose love
She slighted, until e'en her smile were late.—
And may it not be given to hover round
Her pillow, guard where'er she tread, the sacred ground?


## MISCELLANEOUS POEMS

## CHATTERTON TO HIS SISTER

My dearest sister*—smiling child,
May you by phantoms ne'er beguil'd
Your future years, your future life
Spend free from fancy's baneful strife.—
May you ne'er know the pangs I feel.
The grief that acts long past can deal.—
Believe your brother, who has known
To think that visions were his own.
And found how bitter 'twas to form
Such hopes;—better to bear the storm.
Than quiet live away to sleep
A life in dreams we cannot keep;
But which, when reason's magic wand
Shall touch, we wake on desert strand.
With but a memory of all

That rose at fancy's blither call.
Painting to us in brightest hues
All that is flown—for ever flown;
But which our mind still sighing views
In contrast with this scene so lone;
Which nought excites but deep despair,
Instead of hopes—how blithe!—how fair!
Ne'er yield to fancy's wayward flights—
Ne'er, ne'er ascend to fancy's heights,
For great's the fall, and headlong hurl'd
We're scoff'd at, mock'd by all the world.—
I once to fancy thus gave way,
I hail'd, I thought, a glorious day;
I hoped that fame my deeds would crown—
But men o'er all my projects frown.—
What could I poor, unknown expect?—
My hopes my wishes soon were check'd.
And poverty (with visage dire.
With deep sunk eyes of glassy fire.
With teeth choak'd up for want of use.
For e'en the scullion's foul refuse
To her's denied.—With skin that seems
In pity round her clasp'd, it deems
Itself the only link that binds
The living bones, which still it finds.
Will heedless press their galling ends
'Gainst what alone such safety lends.—
With robe, 'tis true—but then the vest
Foul falling rags, with which she's drest,
Won't clothe her limbs, for it would show
The dirtier skin it hides below)
Around me strides whene'er I wake
From dreams but fit for faries' wake.—
But what of this?—these lines the last
My pen shall write, why waste so fast
Upon myself?—I write to thee
To tell thee, how from gloom to flee.

My sister, on your form I gaze.
And soon am lost in thoughtful maze.—
I see your beauty softly rise,
I see your sweet expressive eyes,
I see that dimpled smiling cheek,
I see your face so mildly meek—
And then I think on future hours
When you'll no longer seek for flowers.
Or smiling run with fondest guide,
Along the placid river's side;

Or chasing with a visage sly,
The soaring wanton butterfly.
Fatigued upon her bosom lean—
But through a falsely smiling scene,
I see you thoughtless happy led.
Where fashion flits around your head.
What dangers then beset my dear.
When most the men shall flatter, fear—
When most the men shall softly smile.
They fondly hope they may beguile.
And hope to hurt when most they please.
As vampire bat excites a breeze
Soft, cooling, lulling to repose
The child whose life's blood quickly flows,
Feeding the filthy beast with all
A mother's fondest name may call.

I see your mind will often rest
On flitting image of the breast;
But oh, beware—for as the marsh
Invests the richest hues—no harsh
Unbroken rocks rear high their crests.
But every part a verdure vests
That will invite from browner heath
To flow'ry bog, that spread with death,
Will swallow quick the luckless wight
Who haps upon its breast to light—
Or else, by breathing on the man.
Who midst its snares a path could scan.
Will on him subtle poisons pour
That all his future prospects sour—
For he who drags his poison'd weight.
Diseas'd and rotten while to wait.
He's doom'd for death's long hop'd for dart.
Finds nought to cheer his gleamless heart—
So, so it is with fancy's dream—
It oft shows forms that brightly gleam—
But never dare such forms to clasp.
They'll prove but devils to the grasp,

I see your earnest search for all
That men in men adornments call;
But oh, beware—you hide them well.
For modesty alone must tell
Of what to all by all is given;
Or else, to blush by woman driven
Man soon will hate what first he sought,
And slight, what else his heart had caught.

Ne'er seek to shine by what you know.
For man he loves not what for show
Is form'd alone—but as the glen
Which distance hides from common ken.
By heath, by wildest flower o'erspread,
Bedeck'd alone with shepherd's shed.
Where torrents rush along the vale
And form their winding course through dale,
Is e' en with greater pleasure view'd
Than scene though fair which oft has show'd
Its self-same tints and chequered hues
To eye that tired its stream pursues
With listless gaze, and where in vain.

Extends a rich luxuriant plain,
Where forest nods to sky its head.
Where mix'd are seen the tower and shed.
Where gardens spread before the sight.
Where boundless main, where towering height
The landscape bound—where, rais'd to skies,
The valleys into mountains rise.—
Thus woman's charms, when hid from sight,
If seen by chance, appear more bright.

You see my mood at times so sad,
You see me oft with fury mad.
And oft I've seen your searching eye
To read my darkened brow would try.
You often sought with childish prate
To win your brother from that state—
You often sought to know the cause
That thus my feelings would arouse—
'Twas conscience sting for deeds long done,
When, by a glittering bauble won,
For fame by all from all I sought,
And if for vice a smile I caught,
From wretch—from fool—from worse than fool—
From one of all mankind the tool—
I madly hugg'd myself, and thought
Such fame could not be dearly bought.—
But now 'tis mine to feel the grief,
For which there's nought affords relief—
Though tears will oft o'erflow mine eye.
Still on my heart the load must lie.—
Oft from my heart must burst the sigh.
That grieving hours so slow can fly,—
I think eternity the time
That flows between each length'ning chime,

Telling the slowly wearing hour.—
What heed I life!—Oft, oft the bower
On yonder cliff with flowers o'erspread.
Where violets form a fresh'ning bed.
Where jessamines and roses meet
To shelter them 'gainst scorching heat—
Oft, oft yon bower has shewn to me,
While at its height grew dim my eye—
The softly rising sinking sea
Whither I might for resting fly—
Oft in those waves I've fancied dwelt
Unfound repose for my dark guilt.
And oft I've felt to leap inclin'd—
But then a something to my mind
Would whisper hope—'twill go—
And then my heart would beat more slow—
But no, my heart yet feels the blow
By conscience dealt, and often will
The madd'ning thought return there still.
Then death— but oh! my sister's love
Must still be mine.—'Tis true, I wove
This misery myself.—I heed
It not—but curse not thou the deed.

Farewell, my sister—think of me,
Though far away I fly from thee.—
I love thee so, the hardest thing
My guilt upon my heart could bring.
Is this that now I may not bear
Thy lightsome laughing form so fair
Upon my knee—no, no, a look
From eyes of innocence to brook,
I could not—would not bear.—Farewell.
When thou shalt hear the many tell
Of deeds I've done, by fancy led—
Think how thy brother's heart has bled—
Think how I lov'd thee—do not hate
Thy brother, when thou'rt told his fate,—
Farewell—if prayers from such as me
Could hope. I'd pray alone for thee.

*Chatterton had no sister younger than himself:—the author's imagination has created one for the occasion,—A poetic licence.

TO MRS—

When first I came midst mortals here,
I heard men speak of pleasant dame
Whom oft they sought—but ne'er could hear
More than a voice, which distant came.
Inviting man and woman too
To chase an image of their mind.
As boy, who seems with looks to woo
The bubbles wafted on the wind—
And though his limbs are wearied out
Still chases them with anxious throb.
Till echoing comes th' exultant shout—
But lo! the winds his fancies rob.
Or else the mocking bubble grasp'd
But leaves poor froth within the hand.
He round it hurrying closely clasp'd—
While he faint falls upon the strand—
Or like the fire-fly flitting flame
Lighting all the plants around,
Lures the tir'd traveller, who, lame
With the long weary miles (that wound
Amidst the tangled forest's gloom,
Or changeless desert's wide expanse
Of wand'ring myriads oft the tomb
Prostrate by winds or Arabs' lance)
Still leaves the beaten track in chase
Of this light fairy elfish thing.
Thinking with it his child to grace
If he it to his home can bring—
But when with weary steps he's gone,
Through brake and bush or burning sand,
The sun throws from his Eastern throne
Charm breaking light upon the land,
And leaves what lured him so to roam.
The filthy insect in his sight.
While he falls down thinking of home
Exhausted to eternal night.—
Thus once I ran in search of things
But bubbles of the wanton dame,
Or chas'd such phantoms as had wings
To fly from my too hasty aim—
'Till I at last thought pleasure dwelt
In wildest fancies of the brain,
And thought I inspiration felt
To preach it to the lounging train'—
But since with thee I've sat whole days
And seen thy husband by thee stand,

And children playing in strange ways,
A little merry careless band—
And heard thy loving playful mirth.
First cheer thy husband's toil-worn brow,
Then sooth thy Emma, the last birth
On which thy fond affections grow.—
And since I've heard —'s wiser head
Reason on what he feels so well,
I almost wish like him to tread
The path where such rich pleasures dwell.
And if I thought like thee to find
A wife affectionate and mild.
To all my wayward humours blind—
Who'd sooth my soul as thou thy child—
I'd seek where'er fond hope might lead—
Whatever dangers hovered round,
As long' as aught my hope should feed
I'd never rest—'till she were found.—
But if when gained she show'd a mask,
Had hid a mind as wild as mine.
Oh then to tell sad were the task.
How I should grieve, how I should pine.
For I am not like—; my heart,
My mind by aught but reason led.
Would often feet, would often smart
With bickerings of two wh're wed,
Without perchance a feeling left
That echoing beats in either's breast,—
And then, when thus of hope bereft,
Oh where, where then to seek for rest.—
'Tis better far as now to live,
And even hope for what may ne'er
Perchance be mine, than rashly give
The only stay that keeps me here.—


## ON MAN

Man's restless mind will often seek,
Forgeting that his power is weak,
To soar above, and snatch from heaven
The thunders that to clouds are given—
Boasting himself the lord of all.
He'd have obedient to his call
The hidden stores of earth below
And planets that above him glow—
Would strive to tear the veil that's placed

Before the sphere by Godhead graced.
Forgetful that his mortal eye
Was never form'd to look so high—
Would with despotic slav'ry strive
To chain the power that bade him live.

Who has not often wondering seen
How he with proud and fearless mein.
Will seek new worlds in search of war?
And if he hear but hum afar
Of drum or trumpet's brazen sound,
Will leave e'en wood and favourite hound.
Will even from his children part.
And wife that's nearer to his heart.
And seek an unknown dreadful foe
With sparkling eye and dauntless brow.
Who has not watched the fiery eye
Of man, when first he may espy
The deadly strife of bitter foes—
How with his eyes he follows blows.
How seems t' exult when rushes blood
Bearing of life the sinking flood,
For man, midst murderous war's alarms.
Enjoys the clash of clanging arms,
Is glad to hear the groans around.
Is glad to view the death-strewn ground.
And unmov'd sees the friend of youth
With wounds deform'd, with blood uncouth.
And rushing midst the thickest foes,
Can joy to whet in blood that flows
From husbands—sons—wh're fallen around
From noble warrior's mortal wound;
The sword he from his sire obtain'd
With blood of other ages stain'd.

Who has not seen his cringing bow—
How he will humbly deference show
To those, who'd make him tool for all.
Their lust or folly names may call,
Which make man think the gods could grace
With their own image his dull face.

Who has not seen, with thoughts like these
Seeking his phantasy to please,
How sudden wallowing in lust.
He'll seek to lower e'en his dust—
Give pyramids to harlot's fame,
Divinity to drunkard's name,

Bending: to gods wh're weak in all
But vice, on them devoutly call.
And strive to gain their kindest smile
By what e'en mortals might defile.
Save that their dirt is such—their thought
Might labour long ere 'twould find aught
Below the malice, filth, and dross,
Which laying by in purest loss.
Seeing the beasts some daemon shaped,
And forming man, their image aped.

Why vainly seeks man thus to strive
With will of him who bade him live?
Why seek to shun himself alone
Midst all creation?—Why thus groan
Because no further world remains
To grace his triumphs—wear his chains?
Why, when all beneath his banners bow.
Seeks he where woods their shades may throw
To hide his head midst nature's gloom
And years to restless penance doom?

Thus, always toiling, he can't rest
Till power's robes or penance's vest
Upon his person thrown, appear
To veil the wretch from his own fear.—
Is it that something 'bove this state
Can force him on to seek the great?
'Tis true, he'll tell of higher mind
Below in mortal case confin'd,
Which strives to show itself, though bound.
Above the circumstances round—
But watch him well, let every act.
This passion's slave can here enact.
Be nicely viewed, be nicely weighed,
And all these visions quickly fade.
An infant born perhaps may smile.
Conscious of no intended guile;
And as the single straw may lie
For years corruptless, modestly—
Yet throw that straw upon yon heap,
And quickly, quickly round it creep
Corruption's breath, and putrid air—
Which make it soon what others are—
So infant smiles of innocence
Soon pass away, and every sense
Goes through, midst men, th' intended change
That forms of life the simple range.

And when corruption, rottenness.
Have vested him with all their dress.
Like yonder straw he sinks to earth.
And mingles with what gave him birth.—
It is the consciousness of this
(For modesty may yet be his)
That makes him seek the track of fame.
For she paints other than he came
Into this world, the dying wretch
O'er whom the fiends already stretch
The eager hand to snatch the birth
They'd make the subject of their mirth.


## ON WOMAN

Oh cause of bliss! Oh cause of pain!
Life's only binding pleasing chain!
Amidst life's storms, the only star,
That sheds its cheering light afar.
Alike through times of joy or grief—
Of all our pains the sole relief—
Whose only smile has e'en the pow'r
To smooth the brow, that oft will low'r,—
Whose words will cause the coward heart
To act the brave man's nobler part—
To gain whose smile, the viler seek
To combat death in deserts bleak,
Where whirlwinds raise the sandy plain
Against the Moslam merchant train.
And in one moment sweep away
All trace of man! before how gay!—
To gain whose love, not trophied arch,
Our warrior youth to dangers march;
Undaunted tread the threat'ning deep,
Or forlorn mount the thund'ring steep—
To hear whose lips repeat his name.
The sage will play the statesman's game.
Will seek through danger's tracks untrod—
The name of patriot—name but less than God.—

For with the name of woman's bound
All that below of joy is found—
She softens man by her sweet care,
And mellows all the roughness there.
Oft on the breeze is heard to float
Sweet soothing music's softer note;—

But ne'er the passions of our breast
Like her, will music lull to rest;
She strews the roses in our way,—
And with the names of mother, wife,
She weaves the colours that are gay
In this sad web of mortal life.


## THE CAPTIVES' SONG

### To their Mistress

Though sweet it is to see thee smiling,
And thus our chains our woes beguiling.
And thus old grey hair'd time deceiving,
Sweet pleasure 'midst our woes receiving,
                          In slavery to live.

Still native home such charms possesses,
Still all at home our fancy dresses
In hues so bright, in colours var'ing.
We wish, all fortune's tempests daring.
                          In liberty to live.

For who e'en would in slay'ry feasting
The golden hours of youth be wasting.
If on the rock on heather sleeping.
If in the rill his crust but steeping.
                          He might in freedom live.


## TO ITALY

### Entering by the Simpton, 1816 .

O Italy! at last these vine-clad hills.
The villas' steeples on yon height,
These fertile vales of thousand sparkling rills,
Are thine, and spread before my sight.

No child with hastier step the cot could leave
Of country nurse, its home to seek,
And there a mother's kisses to receive
Upon its rosy colour'd cheek—

Than mine, in anxious search of thee, fam'd land

Where I at least might view the tomb
Of heroes, freemen, patriots, starlike band.
Though now of such thou'rt not the womb.

No friend, nor father, not a mother's tear.
Could bind me to my native shore;
I flew to thee, land! e'en to childhood dear,
For thee their tears unmoved I bore.

Land of my fathers! land by me adored!
Where childhood fix'd its hoped-for joys;
O'er thy historic page my boyhood pored,
And still thy name my thought employs.

Alas! I view thy hills so various deck'd.
Groaning with load of citadel.
Whence barb'rous Huns by all thy charms uncheck'd.
Issuing seek their spoils to swell.

O land! the first in war—in freeman's fame—
Unrivalled yet—when shall I see
Your freeborn hills—your plains of glorious name
Bedeck'd again with liberty?

Lament no more!—See yonder torrents' bed,
The weeds luxuriant spread around;
The thistles, thorns, push forth with haughty head.
Usurp the seeming tranquil ground.

But bursting, breaking, sweeping all away.
The waters wrathful headlong come.
Bearing before in unresisted sway
The heedless revellers to their doom.

Mark yon high crater well! man heedless treads
On its luxuriant sleeping breast,
And proudly on its side his mantle spreads,
And vineyards all its rocks invest.

But see, it comes! it comes! the fiery flood.
And strips the sides of verdure bare;
And laughs at all th' insulting race that stood,
Unconscious of the Godhead there.

E'en thus fair Italy shall raise its head.
Shall pour its strength on their array.
And quick upon the injured shore shall spread
Their blood-like broken sea-waves' spray.

## SONNET

On entering Italy, Sept. 26, 1816

O Italy! are these thy vales?—are these thy mountains
Which oft I painted in my dreams?
Are these thy various winding streams
Which liberty has view'd— are these thy storied fountains?

Yes; here an empire rose—from yonder plain
Issued the warlike band,
That bound in chains this land.
Then dragg'd all tongues, all nations in its train.

Always thou'rt destin'd first midst men to shine—
By God decreed your high renown;
Nor Goth, nor Hun, nor Gaul can undermine—
Always to you remains a crown—
When to the ground your throne by man was hurl'd.
Still by your mitred crown you rul'd the world.


## SONNET

On Buonaparte entering Italy.

Ah! view upon yon Alpine height
The glitt'ring steel, the warriors' state—
Yon echoing cry is freedom's call.
The joyful shout at tyrant's fall.

With smiles Ausonia looks upon her child,
And spreads her richly-gifted land
Before his gaze.—With hope, see! see! she's wild,
That freedom's hers, and by his hand.

But, what! what! rushes on my wilder'd sight?
Ah, Italy! no hope is thine—
Thy son against thee rushes to the fight;
His country's spoils upon him shine—
And thou as peasant sit'st, who's view'd his corn,
By force of clouds he pray'd for, beat down, torn.

## SONNET

On leaving Italy for England, 1817.

O land! whose name on far, far distant shores
Was like that heav'n descended balm,
Which lengthen'd note of mournful organ pours
Through the long aisle our grief to calm.

How oft at eve I gaz'd upon the west,
To view the sun still shining there;
As if thy image glancing on his breast.
Would seek my longing heart to cheer.

As vapours rais'd from distant verdant plain,
Impatient leave the mountain's height.
And sparkling, bounding seek in haste to gain
The vale they think to reach too late:
So have I left Ausonia's wanton strand,
In search of thee, though barren still, my native land.


## SONNET

Written in the Album, at Costessey, after my recovery from an accident, 1817.

Hurl'd from my car I lay upon the ground,
When death, who comes with rapid step alone
To those for whom joy spreads her gleam around,
Ran to transfix the victim 'fore him thrown.
But soon I saw of two fair forms the hands
Outstretch'd in my defence—like those* they seem'd,
Whose breath had caused my happiness—no wands.
No weapons in the air around me gleamed.
Yet death recoil'd—it seemed as if he bowed
Before my guardian's will perchance he thought
He saw in them, as in the two** who brav'd
Awhile his pow'r, the Godhead's image grav'd
So bright; and though majestic, mild it showed.
As if the sov'reign fiat they had brought.

*I had been particularly happy before this accident,
**Adam and Eve in Paradise were not subject to death.

## SONNET

On the same subject.

I Know not how it is—you gave me life!
Yet, can't my heart find words my lips may speak.
In thanks for such a gift?—vain, vain's the strife!
The feeling's strong!—for it all words are weak.—
No muse of Helicon can here avail—
No muse-inspiring god can help me now!
They only aid when fiction forms her tale.
Or give a verse when all but feelings flow.—
Then where to look, if not to him alone,
Who touch'd Isaiah's mouth with burning coal,
If thus he deign'd to touch my lips with fire—
Not then as now—I'd seem a breathing stone;—
But as I feel would speak, and show my soul
Well knows what all your kindness should inspire.

## SONNET

I'm tir'd of this mortality—for years
I scorn'd this nature; for methought I saw
Nought but the marks of virtue caused by fears
Of what the stronger might make into law.
Methought that souls, like the cameleon's skin.
Could every hue invest—the hero, knave,
Or any mask that could a purpose win.
Or help the various plot of passion's slave.
And now that I have found some who perform
The noblest acts, not for the use alone,
But that their natures form'd in virtue's mould.
I scorn mortality, which cannot form
A word worthy of virtue's heavenly throne.
At such a sight my feeling's to unfold.

## SONNET

To Wm. Taylor, Jun. of Norwich, leaving him in 1815

Though fates may by their dread decree
Part friends, and snatch thee from my sight;
Yet, can't they touch my memory,
Which oft will bring back past delight?

And oft when grief or sadness weigh
Upon thy friend's desponding soul,
The thoughts of hours with thee, how gay!
I from these haggard beldames stole,
Will smooth the furrows of my cheek.
And gild reflecting back past joy.
The hour that flies without relief,—
To griefs I've suffer'd from a boy.—
Thus, though we part, in thought you near shall
Your image still shall act the friend to me.


## SONNET

I wander now along the sea-beat shore.
Where bending like misfortune, seem
The towering rocks o'er waves that joy no more,
From which they hide the moon's bright gleam—
While happy others rippling sportive play
Their flitting course with smiles is blest.
But not long thus, for soon th' apparel gay
Is lost, and soon they sink to rest.
And often here an envious current drives
The once so happy wave in turn
To darkness and to shade,—In vain it strives;
It cannot fate's decree o'erturn,—
Fit emblem of mankind, whom fortune's smile,
Though vain as moon's pale light, will oft of ill beguile.


## SONNET

What though a waste of dark green waves
Shall flow between my love and me;
'Tis nought, the foam which ocean paves.
Shall serve to bear my thought to thee.

What though the Alps with snowy vest
Shall stand between thy feet and mine;
The eagle of the cloud-capt nest.
Shall fly and bear my thought to thine.

And though e'en time should interpose
Between my heart and its desire;
'Tis nought—the breast that for thee glows,

an never feel another's fire;
or can e'en thought e'er find repose.
ave when with thee whom I admire.


SONNET

To my Book.

Farewell! farewell! the hopes Eve built on thee
Will fail too like the rest.—I heed it not.
Far bitt'rer pangs than thou canst give to me,
I've borne withal.—Though such may be thy lot,
I will no more revile thee, than the sire
His son, though graceless he may prove, and leave
His grey hairs hopeless.—No; whate'er my lyre
Has sung, thou hast; thou chronicler of grief!
And I shall be most glad to read thy page
When memory lags, and life is lost in age;
Though thou mayst tell of hope for ever gone.
Of heart that wither'd finds itself alone
Midst crowds,—a stranger midst its friends,
To which its sympathy no being lends.

www.ingramcontent.com/pod-product-compliance
Lightning Source LLC
Chambersburg PA
CBHW060034050426
42448CB00012B/3010